Walk!

Dartmoor

with

Kate & Alan Hobbs

DISCOVERY WALKING GUIDES LTD

Walk! Dartmoor
First Edition - January 2006
Copyright © 2006

Published by
Discovery Walking Guides Ltd
10 Tennyson Close, Northampton NN5 7HJ, England

Mapping supplied by **Global Mapping Limited**
(www.globalmapping.com)

 This product includes mapping data licensed from **Ordnance Survey®** with the permission of the Controller of Her Majesty's Stationery Office. © Crown Copyright 2005. All rights reserved.
Licence Number 40044851

Photographs
All photographs in this book were taken by the authors.
Front Cover Photographs

Headland Warren Farm
(Walk 11)

Bowerman's Nose
(Walk 13)

Lustleigh Cleave
(Walk 17)

Tavy Cleave
(Walk 5)

ISBN 1-904946-12-7
Text and photographs* © Kate & Alan Hobbs

Walk!
Dartmoor

CONTENTS

THE WALKS

THE AUTHORS

Alan and Kate, engineer and teacher have lived happily and quietly between Bristol and Bath raising a family for nigh on 30 years.

Cycling, sailing and walking helped to keep them sane but they finally decided that enough was enough and escaped the rat race to pursue their own interests full time. They jumped at the opportunity to become researchers for DWG after discovering Walk! Tenerife which got them off the beach and into the hills and they haven't looked back since. Their 'Gap life' is proving very successful with walking, the major part, being interspersed with frequent jaunts abroad tracking down their itinerant son!

Dedication
For Ewan

Acknowledgements

To Ros and David for their steady support, guidance and encouragement throughout this venture; to the Dartmoor National Park Authority for much help and advice; to Helen and John for their local knowledge, library and excellent company and to Jill and Eric for the loan of their dog, Duncan.

INTRODUCTION

"Why on earth are we going out today?"
This question crossed our minds more than once when setting out to research this book, with the wind howling, a good chance of mist on the bleak *tors* and treacherous mires waiting to suck us in. And if myth and legend are anything to go by, the Devil or at least his pack of bloodthirsty hounds would be after us to really make our day!

But then, there are those crystal clear, sunny days when there's no such questioning, when there's no better place to be than Dartmoor; glorious views, wide-open spaces and an overwhelming sense of freedom. Whatever the weather Dartmoor obliges, promising an exhilaration hard to match, a great sense of adventure and a wonderful tranquillity of spirit. We think it has to do with its rugged hilltops, spectacular gorges and idyllic river valleys coupled with stunning flora and fauna and, as if that's not enough, history greets us at almost every turn. The forty walks in this book allow you to explore and enjoy all these faces of Dartmoor, secure in the knowledge that you'll get home unscathed and enriched.

THE LANDSCAPE

Dartmoor granite

Dartmoor's 365 square miles of natural beauty lie within the heart of Devon, one of southern England's largest areas of exposed granite. 280 million years ago the area was totally submerged beneath the sea, covered with a thick layer of sedimentary sandstone, slate and shale which was then squeezed and buckled into new mountains with molten granite rising up behind it, baking and compressing the surrounding rocks into metamorphic limestone and marble.

The sea retreated about 65 million years ago and erosion by wind and water started to wear away the sedimentary covering of shale and chalk to reveal the hard granite core. The tropical, forested landscape then became home to an abundance of mammals and insects. Much remained the same until about half a million years ago the climate changed with the first of four ice ages. Dartmoor was frozen, buried in snow and ice which broke down the granite forming its characteristic rocky *tors* and *clitter* slopes. A mere 10 thousand years ago a climate similar to today's developed, bringing with it forests of oak, hazel and elm with deer, wolf, wild boar and oxen and the first prehistoric people leaving their mark on the moor. **Wistman's Wood** is one of the few remaining areas of carefully conserved upland oakwood, hinting at what Dartmoor was once like (Walk 8).

MAN'S INFLUENCE

Little evidence remains of the earliest nomadic Dartmoor inhabitants, the chambered tomb known as **Spinsters' Rock** near **Castle Drogo** being a notable exception. By 2000 BC much of the forested area of the moor had been cleared and the high ground which was covered with a thick layer of peat

became water logged, an ideal place for sphagnum moss to survive, turning into the characteristic Blanket Bog which covers about 100 square miles of high Dartmoor today (Walk 8). As farming techniques developed, so did more permanent stone-built settlements, such as at **Grimspound** (Walk 12) and **Kestor** (Walk 24) along with ceremonial sites including numerous stone rows, standing stones and burial cairns, seen for example, at **Merrivale** (Walks 7, 27) and **Drizzlecombe** (Walk 29).

Thousands of such remains survive, all dating from the Bronze Age. At its peak around 1500 BC, it is estimated that the moor supported several thousand inhabitants but this population gradually declined, probably due to worsening weather and overworked soil. By the start of the Iron Age (700 BC) the upland moor was mainly deserted and remained so until Saxon times, there being little evidence of any Roman influence - but by medieval times (roughly 550-1550 AD) things started looking up!

Bennett's Cross

Farming became widespread, the churches were powerful and land ownership grew increasingly important through the Middle Ages, three wealthy abbeys at **Tavistock**, **Buckfast** and **Buckland** wielding influence until their dissolution during Henry V111's reign. The first known attempt to set the boundary of the common grazing land central to Dartmoor, the **Forest of Dartmoor**, was a perambulation around its borders in about 1240 - a walk or horse-ride of approximately 50 miles. Boundary stones and granite crosses commonly marked parishes, land ownership and warrens and also served as route markers for safe tracks across the moor.

An abundance of these handsome stones and crosses survive today, their markings providing fascinating clues to their past history. The routes known today as **Lich Way** (Walk 8), **Abbot's Way** (Walk 40) and the route between **Tavistock** and **Ashburton** (Walk 27) were well known, crossing not only bleak moor but streams and rivers, so fording water was quite an issue! Stepping stones were a help but clapper bridges, constructed from massive slabs of granite supported at each end, sometimes on a central pier as at **Postbridge** (Walk 10), were designed to ease the way across and still provide

West Dart stepping stones

many a well-known and much loved landmark.

Ollsbrim Longhouse

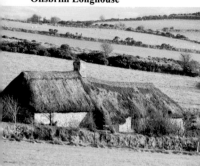

Communities thrived and were decimated during this period; about a third of the population died as a result of the Black Death in 1348 resulting in the desertion of many settlements, but the moor still tells much of how people lived and worked in those times. Longhouses were characteristic dwelling places where man and beast shared accommodation; more than a hundred remain on Dartmoor today - the site at **Hound Tor** is particularly evocative (Walk 14).

Sheep, goats and cattle were farmed together with some crops and evidence of this agriculture endures even now - strip *lynchets*, narrow terraces on hillslopes, can be picked out at **Challacombe Down** (Walk 11). Rabbits were bred widely on Dartmoor for food and fur (Walks 11 and 29), a typical warren consisting of pillow mounds, large cigar shaped piles of earth for rabbits to burrow into easily, with vermin traps to pick off stoats and weasels together with accommodation for farmers and dogs.

INDUSTRIAL DARTMOOR

Dartmoor has a long and profitable association with tin mining, the first written record of its extraction on Dartmoor being dated at 1156 AD. Originally 'streaming' took place (rather like panning for gold) in streams and rivers, followed later by open working, where deep horizontal cuts known as adits were made into the hillside to follow the lode. Examples of these workings can be clearly seen at the sites of the **Birch Tor** and **Vitifer** mines (Walk 11). Once extracted the tin ore (casserite) was taken to the water powered blowing house where it was crushed and smelted, the resulting ingots then being transported to one of the Stannary towns, **Ashburton**, **Chagford**, **Tavistock** and **Plympton** for assaying. But the commercial exploitation of Dartmoor minerals started in earnest in the 18th century when tin, copper and lead were extracted from the moor, followed later by granite used for building and china clay destined for bricks, pipes and pottery.

Granite had been used locally on Dartmoor since ancient times as a building material; however it was not until the late 18th century that quarrying became a commercial venture as demand increased due to town development, notably at **Plymouth** nearby. The granite was worked from surface deposits until 1780 when quarrying started at **Haytor** (Walks 14, 16) as a result of contract won to rebuild London Bridge. The **Foggintor** and **Swelltor** quarries began production in the 1820s (Walk 27) transporting their stone to **Plymouth** by railway; Nelson's Column was built from **Foggintor** stone.

Foggintor Quarry

Merrivale quarry (Walk 7) opened later and was worked continually until 1997. One of its last commissions was to provide stone for the War Memorial on the Falklands.

Extraction of china clay, predominantly in south-west Dartmoor, began in the mid 19th century. Remains of old quarries and resulting spoil heaps of sand and mica are found at several locations, most notably at **Red Lake** (Walk 40). Peat, another Dartmoor commodity, was used over a long period, though there's little visible evidence of its extraction.

Devonport Leat

However, the course of the tramway from the **Rattlebrook Peatworks** to **Bridstowe** can still be traced (Walk 4). All this activity lead to the construction of a supporting infrastructure for the transport of people and goods, thus also improving communication between communities. *Leats* were constructed, collecting and transporting water for use as domestic supply and to power mills and mines. Perhaps the most famous, the **Devonport Leat** (Walks 26, 29, 30) was constructed in 1790 to provide the booming **Devonport** dockyard with water, today terminating at **Burrator Reservoir**.

Many tramways were used to transport granite, clay and peat off the moor and interesting remains can be seen at **Haytor** (Walk 16), **Redlake** (Walks 33, 40) and **Swelltor** quarries, where parts of the old tramway were subsumed into the **Princetown Railway** (Walk 27). Railways really came to Dartmoor in the mid-19th century with lines encircling the moor; today the only remaining routes are operated as tourist attractions, such as the picturesque **Dart Valley Railway** and the **Dartmoor Railway** which takes visitors to the impressive **Meldon Viaduct** (Walk 2).

Farming still survives, but tourism is a significant industry on Dartmoor today. So - what to do on Dartmoor apart from walking? Rock climbing, cycling, canoeing, fishing, horse riding and letterboxing are readily at hand, with plenty of inviting pubs and tempting cream tea shops nearby to lure you from the path of righteousness.

Bluebells

Dartmoor is rich in flora and fauna, having several of its own particular specialities. Upland oak woods are home to an abundance of lichen and mosses, St. John's Wort and the insectivorous sundew have their own hideaways while fields, lanes and pathways play host to stunning displays of daffodils, bluebells, primroses, orchids and many other wild flowers. Apart from the ubiquitous sheep and cattle, Dartmoor is home to a few snakes, a great variety of birds (warbler, dipper, curlew, buzzard and more) and some gorgeous butterflies, damselflies and dragonflies.

A cute Dartmoor resident

The otter is currently regaining territory and salmon and seatrout do a good job keeping down the insect population on the rivers. But Dartmoor is perhaps most famous for its ponies, casually wandering across moor and road alike, always seemingly blissfully unaware of any traffic and just enjoying life.

THE WALKS

We've included a variety of walks around most of the moor – high moor, gentle riverside, country lane/bridlepath to suit a range of weathers and fitness levels. And there's always at least one point of interest – it might be a spectacular view, some ancient remains or traces of bygone industries but the countryside in its own right will always be worth the effort of rugging up and getting out. The longest walk is 11 miles/17 kilometres and the shortest 4 miles/6½ kilometres. Many of the longer routes offer shortcuts or strolls as alternatives, so you can tailor the route on the day depending on mood or weather. Some walks can be linked together to give more variety and challenge (e.g. Walks 10&36, 17&18, 29&30). Pure walking times vary from 4¼ to 1¾ hours but of course you may not walk at our speed - try out a couple of routes to get a feel for how your pace corresponds with ours and adjust your timings accordingly. We haven't allowed for any stopping times on the way so be prepared to build in extra minutes for lazing, grazing or gazing.

PRESERVING THE ENVIRONMENT

Cars

Dartmoor is bounded by the A30 to the north and the A38 to the south with just one real 'transmoor' road that crosses it. Other routes are mainly charmingly pretty but narrow (and therefore slow) country lanes - be prepared to reverse! Buses and trains can make life simpler; see the appendices for details.

Parking in moorland car parks and in some settlements can be limited, particularly during peak holiday periods. Please park sensibly with consideration for local residents and where possible use public transport.

Dogs

Dogs should be kept under control at all times to protect farm animals or wildlife. Please keep your dog on a short lead between 1 March and 31 July to avoid worrying lambs and ewes and disturbing ground nesting birds, and all year round near farm animals.

Birds

During the bird breeding season (March to July) please keep to tracks and paths as much as possible particularly in areas of dense heather, *clitter* and wetlands.

Where you can walk - Access Opportunities on Dartmoor.

The vast areas of open country on north and south Dartmoor (35,200 hectares) are mainly common land. Generally speaking, access is unrestricted on foot and horseback (except for Firing Ranges). In addition, the National Park Authority has secured public access to certain other areas on foot, by agreement with a number of landowners/occupiers. There are also other permitted areas, for example Forestry Commission woodlands and some National Trust land. Some areas of open country are also accessible under the Countryside & Rights of Way Act (CROW Act) and the Dartmoor National Park Authority provides access points to such land - look out for these logos.

The right of access is for walkers only and, may be restricted; for example, landowners have the right to close their land for up to 28 days a year.

www.countrysideaccess.gov.uk   www.dartmoor-npa.gov.uk
www.openaccess.gov.uk

FIRING RANGES

The Ministry of Defence has a training area on northern Dartmoor, which comprises three live firing ranges (**Okehampton**, **Merrivale** and **Willsworthy**). The public has access to these moorland areas, the boundaries of which are marked by a series of red and white posts, **except when the ranges are used for live firing.** When you wish to enter one (or more) of the ranges you must check the firing times and you must heed any warning signals (red flags by day and red lamps at night). As Dartmoor has been used for military training since the early 1800s, there's always a risk that you could come across strange items or metal objects - don't touch them! Mark and note the location and inform the 'Commandant, **Okehampton Camp**' or the police.

You have guaranteed access to the ranges on public holidays and 1-31 August inclusive, but for all other times the firing programme must be consulted. It is published in local newspapers, at Information Centres and is available on freephone, 0800 458 4868 (currently) and www.dartmoor-ranges.co.uk. When there's no live firing, training may still be taking place. Don't be worried if you see pyrotechnics or hear firing - they're blanks.

Note: on post 2005 OS Dartmoor Explorer Maps each Range Danger Area is shown individually and symbolised by inward facing solid red triangles. Even though there is no yellow background tint (which is used on the maps to depict access land) public access is available at specified times - see above.

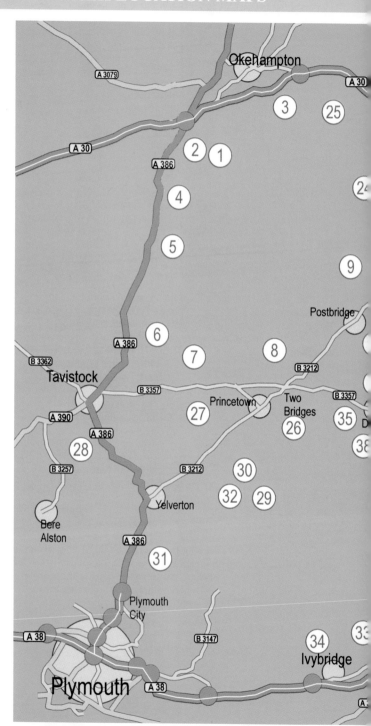

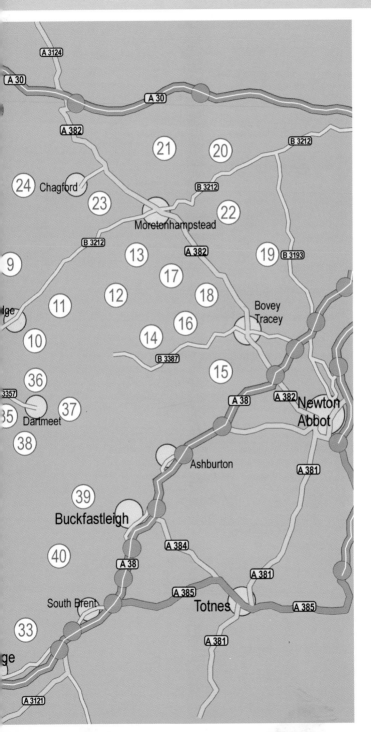

SYMBOLS RATING GUIDE

 3 our rating for effort/exertion:-
1 very easy **2** easy **3** average
4 energetic **5** strenuous

 2½ H approximate **time** to complete
a walk (compare your times
against ours early in a walk) -
does not include stopping time

 5 miles/8km approximate walking
distance in
miles/kilometres

250m approximate
ascents/descents in
850m metres (N=negligible)

circular route   **linear** route   **figure of eight** route   risk of **vertigo**

 3 **refreshments** (may be at start or end of a route only)

- Walk descriptions include:
- timing in minutes, shown as (40M)
- compass directions, shown as (NW)
- heights in metres, shown as (1355m)
- GPS waypoints, shown as (Wp.3)

Notes on the text
Place names are shown in **bold text**,
except where we refer to a written
sign, when they are enclosed in single
quotation marks. Local or unusual
words are shown in *italics*, and are
explained in the accompanying text.

ORDNANCE SURVEY MAPPING

All the map sections which accompany the detailed walk descriptions in
Walk! Dartmoor are reproduced under Ordnance Survey licence from the
digital versions of the latest Explorer 1:25,000 scale maps. Each map section
is re-scaled to the 40,000 scale used in DWG's Walk!/Walks series of guide
books. Walking Route and GPS Waypoints are then drawn onto the map
section to produce the map illustrating the detailed walk description.

Walk! Dartmoor's map sections are sufficient to follow the detailed walk
descriptions, but for planning your adventures in this region, and if you want
to divert from the walking routes, we strongly recommend that you purchase
the latest OS Explorer maps.

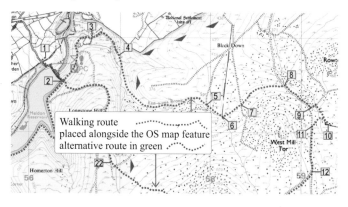

Walking route
placed alongside the OS map feature
alternative route in green

The GPS Waypoint lists provided in this book are as recorded by Alan and Kate Hobbs while researching the detailed walk descriptions. Waypoint symbols are numbered so that they can be directly identified with the walk description and waypoint list. All GPS Waypoints are subject to the accuracy of GPS units in the particular location of each waypoint.

Satellite Reception

Accurate location fixes for your GPS unit depend upon you receiving signals from four or more satellites. Providing you have good batteries, and that you wait until your GPS has full 'satellite acquisition' before starting out, your GPS will perform well in Dartmoor. Where Alan and Kate encountered poor satellite reception it is mentioned in the walk description.

Manually Inputting Waypoints

GPS Waypoints are quoted for the OSGB (Ordnance Survey Great Britain) datum and BNG (British National Grid) coordinates, making them identical with the OS grid coordinates of the position they refer to. To manually input the Waypoints into your gps we suggest that you:

- switch on your GPS and select 'simulator/standby' mode
- check that your GPS is set to the OSGB datum and BNG 'location/position format'
- input the GPS Waypoints into a 'route' with the same number as the walking route; then when you call up the 'route' in Dartmoor there will be no confusion as to which walking route it refers
- repeat the inputting of waypoints into routes until you have covered all the routes you plan to walk, or until you have used up the memory capacity of your GPS
- turn off your GPS. When you turn your GPS back on it should return to its normal navigation mode.

Note that GPS Waypoints complement the routes in Walk! Dartmoor, and are not intended as an alternative to the detailed walking route descriptions.

Personal Navigator Files (PNFs) CD version 3.01

Edited versions of Alan and Kate's original GPS research tracks and waypoints are available as downloadable files on our PNFs CD, which also includes all the edited GPS tracks and waypoints for all the Walk!/Walks guide books published by DWG along with GPS Utility Special Edition software. See DWG websites for more information:

www.walking.demon.co.uk & www.dwgwalking.co.uk

GPS The Easy Way (£4.99)

If you are confused by talk of GPS, but are interested in how this modern navigational aid could enhance your walking enjoyment, then simply seek out a copy of GPS The Easy Way, the UK's best selling GPS manual.

Here's our personal list of walking gear:

- a decent sized waterproof **backpack** (25-30 litre) big enough to hold spare clothing, food and drink with several side pockets (with robust zips) for the extras
- the walking can be rough so strong, waterproof **walking boots** that will give you support and a good grip on rocks and slippery slopes are recommended. Comfortable **socks** are a must and **gaiters** come in handy when tramping over the wetter areas.
- we go for **layers** (with any spare layers in a plastic bag in the backpack) as the weather varies and can change very quickly. A **quick drying shirt** or **T-shirt** and a **fleece** (a spare warm jumper for the cold-blooded), and a **hat** and **gloves** in a side pocket. A good quality **waterproof jacket** is essential (a lighter weight one in summer) together with **waterproof trousers**
- an adjustable **walking pole** for extra support and balance
- a small kit with **plasters**, **bandage**, **sunscreen**, **fly repellent**, **bite soothing cream** and **antiseptic cream** - and it's worth checking for ticks on your return. A **whistle** and **torch** can be useful
- a small **bottle of water** each (500 ml) is usually enough for English weather. We usually take a **packed lunch** (if we're not stopping at a pub en route) and survival rations; **dried fruit and nuts** are good, tropical mix being our current favourite.
- do not compromise. Buy the best **guidebook** and the best **map** (in a waterproof case) and carry them with you. Mists and bogs are hazards on Dartmoor and thus navigational tools are essential. A **compass** is useful to orientate yourself and for general directions, but a **GPS unit** is far more useful - see Using GPS on Dartmoor.

Safety Guidelines

Dartmoor is stunningly beautiful but it can be hazardous. Here are a few hints.

Before you set out:

- check the weather - it's very changeable on Dartmoor. Weathercall 09014 722054 www.meto.gov.uk
- check the firing times - see page 13
- check our guidance on walking equipment - see above
- let someone know the route you're taking - mobile phone reception is poor so you can't rely on phone contact
- unless you are experienced, don't walk alone in remote country
- allow plenty of time and daylight to complete each walk. The timings given in this book are 'pure' walking times

While you are out:

- always know exactly where you are. Mist is a frequent hazard on Dartmoor; you can lose sight of landmarks very quickly.
- stay on the route; retrace your steps if it becomes impassable.
- if the weather deteriorates consider your options; do not hesitate to turn back.
- keep away from all moorland livestock.
- if in doubt about crossing a river find a bridge or crossing point, or go upstream until the river is easier to cross. If necessary retrace your steps off the moor.

1 DARTMOOR'S HIGHEST TORS - YES TOR & HIGH WILLHAYS

Choose a clear day for this expedition so you can fully appreciate the tremendous views from Dartmoor's highest peaks. The walk starts at **Meldon Reservoir** and follows the **Red-a-ven Brook** up onto the moor. We skirt round **West Mill Tor**, creeping up on **Yes Tor** peak from the south, discovering on the way a small hidden lake and disused military railway. **High Willhays** (Dartmoor's highest peak), is our next destination, from where we descend to the **West Okement River** valley and mysterious **Black-a-tor Copse** on the return path to the reservoir.

Safety Advice: Please note that live firing frequently takes place on **Okehampton Range**. It is imperative to check the Firing Times before undertaking this walk. See the section on Dartmoor Firing Ranges in the introduction.

5 | 4¼ H | 11 miles/17 km | 400m / 400m | 0

Shortcut
From the trig point on **Yes Tor** (Wp.14), head on a bearing 290 degrees down towards **Meldon Reservoir** following sheep tracks over the rough ground to meet a track at Wp.22. Turning right, skirt the east side of **Longstone Hill** to rejoin the main route as it makes its way back across the dam (2¾ hours, 7 miles/11km).

Access by car: take the B3260 heading west from **Okehampton**. After 2½ miles, cross the A30 and continue straight on to **Meldon**. Through the village, turn left after the bridge and head to the 'Reservoir Car Park'.

We leave the car park (Wp.1 0M) and head left up the lane towards **Meldon Reservoir**, then cross the dam; there are impressive views to the right and left of the reservoir and deep valley which leads to **Meldon** quarries and viaduct.

Over the dam (Wp.2 5M), we immediately turn left and through a small gate (ignoring the gate leading to the spillway) onto a narrow gravel track contouring round the hillside with **West Okement River** in the valley on our left.

Looking back we see the dam with a curtain of water cascading down when the reservoir is full, producing fascinating moving patterns on the smooth concrete. After 400 yards we meet a broad grassy track and turn left downhill, keeping left at a fork, to old aplite quarry workings and a bridge across **Red-a-ven Brook** (Wp.3 15M).

Meldon dam

The disused quarries near **Meldon** dam, worked from the 1880s until the 1920s, extracted aplite, a mineral used to produce distinctive pale green glass manufactured close by. Only fragments of broken glass can be found here as all whole bottles and jars have long since been carried off.

Red-a-ven Brook

We cross the brook and turn right. The path winds its way up the valley for 500 yards with the stream tumbling down on our right, when we fork right off the main track (Wp.4 21M), still following the **Red-a-ven** valley gently up towards the high moor.

Red-a-ven Reservoir

We cross a small stream coming from our left and continue across rough grassland and the occasional boggy stretch, following sheep tracks with **Yes Tor** dominating the skyline ahead, gradually veering east and climbing more steeply until we cross a military track (Wp.5 45M). Still following the stream, we discover the small disused **Red-a-ven** reservoir (Wp.6 49M) languishing beneath a small terrace, water spilling over from one corner.

From the reservoir we head north-east, contouring round the north side of **West Mill Tor** across very rough ground - even the sheep find it difficult to head in a straight line here! We cross another military track (Wp.7 53M) continuing (NE) to an intersection with a tarmac road coming from **Okehampton Camp** on the left (Wp.8 62M) where we turn right. The road climbs steadily, swinging to the right round the slopes of **West Mill Tor** to reach a track on the left heading off to the bunkers of a firing range (Wp.9 67M). For railway enthusiasts, a short diversion turning left on the track then right along the back of an earth mound brings us to a 300 yard section of narrow gauge track (Wp.10 72M), an engine shed at one end and a turning circle at the other. The railway was used for moving targets across the firing range, and though now disused, a locomotive can still be seen through the cracks of the locked doors of the shed.

Retracing our steps, we cut across left over a small stream back onto the main track (Wp.11 82M) and turn left (S), following this stony track. We bear right (SW) at a fork (Wp.12 88M) up onto the saddle between **Yes Tor** and **High Willhays** (Wp.13 109M) where we turn right on the track up to the **Yes Tor** trig point (Wp.14 113M).

The summit rewards us with spectacular views, so take a well-earned rest and admire the wonderful vistas. **High Willhays**, our next destination, is reputedly higher by 7 feet - both *tors* are the only ones on Dartmoor over 2000 feet.

To the north the rolling country side of central and north Devon unfolds, while to the south we look over the remoter parts of Dartmoor, the cairn on **High Willhays** clearly visible, though from this view point it looks distinctly lower than we are!

We set off south, retracing our steps on the well-trodden peaty path heading for **High Willhays** (Wp.15 126M) - surprisingly, **Yes Tor** still looks higher! Did they get it wrong? From this point our route must be down! And we continue, following the well-used track through the coarse moorland grass, heading south-east and gently downhill to **Dinger Tor** (Wp.16 142M). On our right the rocky outcrops of **Lints Tor** are visible as we head across the moorland (S) down the spur from **Dinger Tor**, then bend right, contouring round the head of a small valley before climbing to the silhouetted rocks of **Lints Tor** (Wp.17 160M).

There's plenty of shelter from the wind, and excellent views down the steep sided valley and the meandering **West Okement River** from here. Our path heads from the *tor* (NW), down to the valley and keeps to the right hand side of the river. We soon pick up a track which hugs the foot of the hillside, avoiding boggy areas in the river flood plain.

As the valley narrows we enter **Black-a-tor Copse** (Wp.18 186M), a National Nature Reserve containing an area of high altitude oak woodland. The moss and lichen covered trees are gnarled and stunted, pushing up out of the boulder-strewn ground.

Black-a-Tor Copse

The path follows the river bank closely as we make our way through the trees, emerging into an open well grazed area (Wp.19 202M), a perfect spot for a picnic.

Our riverside path becomes very wet as we divert right around a small reservoir, but soon turns into a track as we start descending more steeply, the river rushing into a gorge on the left. As we reach the end of the valley the track curves right, and we see a footbridge on the left crossing a side stream (Wp.20 224M). A fenced area ahead marks the start of **Meldon Reservoir** and we make our way round on the right hand side, following the well-trodden path back to **Meldon** dam, from where we retrace our steps to the car park (Wp.21 249M).

2 SOURTON & BRANSCOMBE'S LOAF

This area of Dartmoor is fascinating for its wealth of industrial archaeology; this walk takes in viaducts, railway and mining with plenty of opportunities to ponder and explore. A brisk climb leads to expansive views of Dartmoor's highest peaks and far beyond and is followed by a mellow stroll alongside a tranquil reservoir. If you fancy a little detour to **Sourton** on the way - the church is charming, the cross and old post office are fascinating and the pub - well, just take a look!

Short Walk
(2 hours, 5 miles/8km)

Follow the route to Wp.10 looking down at the ford crossing the small stream. Instead of zigzagging downhill, head (SW) on a small grassy track, contouring to meet the stream higher up and then following its course onwards uphill. Cross one track and then another (Wp.20) and continue along the dry stream bed heading onto the saddle between **Corn Ridge** and **Sourton Tors**. Turn sharp right (Wp.21) almost back on yourself on a level track behind the **Tors**. As the route descends you'll come to a row of standing stones and the curious remains of an old ice works. Continuing downhill between two stone posts (Wp.22), fork left off the main track (N) dropping steadily to the car park (Wp.19).

To quote the splendid W.I. information board,

"In the 19th century there was a thriving industry on the north side of **Sourton Tors** producing ice. During the hard winters water was piped from a spring into an ice shed. When frozen it was removed from the tanks, laid in blocks in shallow beds which you can still see and covered with turf for insulation. In the warm weather the blocks were taken by horse and cart to the cities for the preservation of food, notably at fish markets. The remains of the buildings and beds are still evident."

Access by car:
From **Okehampton** heading south-west on the A30, take the A386 turn towards **Tavistock** and **Sourton**, then take the second small turning on the left signed to the 'Granite Way & Lydford' cycle track. Park immediately on the left.

We leave the carpark (Wp.1 0M) and join the **Granite Way** heading (SW) towards **Sourton**. Easy strolling takes us under **Lavis Bridge** and then on to a green metal signpost by **Sourton Church** (Wp.2 11M) where we leave the cycle track to the right up to a wooden gate. Turning right through the gate would take us on a short diversion to the church and **Highwayman Inn**; otherwise we turn left crossing the **Granite Way**.

Through a second gate we come to the moor in a grassy corridor between stone walls. On reaching open land (Wp.3 20M) we turn right on a level track parallel to a wall, with **Sourton Tors** rising steeply to our left. After 600 yards, as the wall bears away to the right (Wp.4 29M), we join a track turning left and start to climb, swinging round the base of the spur.

The spectacular 'Deep Valley' appears to our right as do good views of the handsome **Lake Viaduct** that used to carry the Southern Railway until 1968. At the head of the valley a boundary stone (Wp.5 43M) marks a crossing points of tracks - we don't take any of these!

We go south-east on an indistinct sheep track across rough grassland aiming for a rocky outcrop on the top of **Corn Ridge**. After 200 yards we cross a wide track (Wp.6 46M), part of the old road between **Okehampton** and **Lydford**, and continue the steep ascent up **Corn Ridge**, aiming for the cairn at the highest point (Wp.7 62M).

The Legend of Branscombe's Loaf

Back in the 13th century, as Walter Bronescombe (Bishop of Exeter), was riding home from **Tavy** with his chaplain Reg they were caught in bad weather and became tired and hungry. They met a friendly stranger on **Corn Ridge** who offered them bread and cheese, but just before the Bishop began to eat Reg knocked the loaf from his hand - he noticed that the stranger had cloven hooves, a sure sign of Satan. The Devil fled and the loaf and cheese became the granite boulders now known as **Branscombe's Loaf**.

Impressive views open up with distant glimpses of the sea off **Plymouth Sound** to the south and, closer, views of **Meldon Reservoir** and **Lake Viaduct**. We continue east towards the unmistakable outline of **Branscombe's Loaf** (Wp.8 64M) from where we look across the **West Okement** river valley to **Yes Tor** and **High Willhays**,

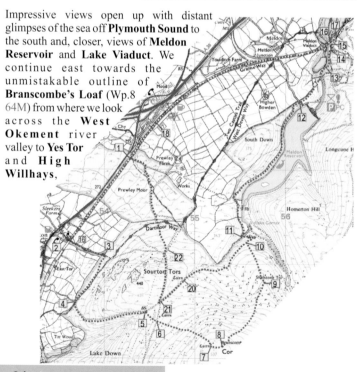

the highest points on Dartmoor.

Our path takes us downhill (NE) towards the southern tip of **Meldon Reservoir**, and avoiding the marshy patches, we make for **Shelstone Tor** (Wp.9 77M) - an excellent sheltered spot for a refreshment stop.

Fording the side stream at Wp.11

We head (NNW) down the spur towards **Vellake Corner**, initially picking our way through the *clitter*. As we approach the river the terrain becomes increasingly steep and on meeting a small track (Wp.10 84M) we can clearly see our path zigzagging down to a ford at a side stream (Wp.11 87M).

Meldon Reservoir

Over the stream, we head through a gate signed 'Reservoir Walks and Meldon carpark' to follow a picturesque path along the reservoir contouring around its north-west side.

Across the access road to the dam (Wp.12 110M) we go through a small wooden gate onto a bridlepath to **Meldon Viaduct**.

The path descends to river level through woods alongside a flooded quarry on the left taking us to a wooden footbridge across the river on the right (Wp.13 121M). Over the bridge we turn immediately left on a narrow gravel path through spoil heaps and past disused quarry buildings, admiring the massive **Meldon Viaduct** in all its glory. A wooden gate (Wp.14 124M) leads us up into trees and after 100 yards we cross the **Meldon Quarry** access road onto a yellow waymarked footpath up and under the viaduct (Wp.15 125M). Steep steps bring us to a gravel path (Wp.16 127M) where we turn right zigzagging precipitously up onto the viaduct (Wp.17 130M).

The views of **Meldon Valley** and dam from here are stunning and there is plenty of interest at the **Dartmoor Railway Visitor Centre** where, at weekends and during the summer season, refreshments are available. For our return we go left (SW) on the **Granite Way** across the viaduct enjoying a gentle stroll, (passing a refreshment stop at **The Prewley Moor Arms**, for which fork right at Wp.18 157M, past the **Bundu Caravan Site**) back to the car park (Wp.19 162M).

3 EAST OKEMENT RIVER & BELSTONE TOR

This walk starts in the area of the restored **Okehampton Railway Station** and **Dartmoor Information Centre** and takes us down into the breathtaking **East Okement River** valley, from where we climb steadily alongside the cascading river up to the open moor. The route then takes us past the magical **Nine Maidens** stone circle down to the fascinating river crossing at **Cullever Steps** and then, admiring the historic **Irishman's Wall**, we climb **Higher Tor** and descend to the **River Taw** valley. We conclude the walk via beautiful **Belstone Village**, see the old stocks and maybe take refreshment at the pub before returning once again to **Okehampton**.

3	3H	9 miles/14 km		250m 250m		3

Stroll	**Shortcut**
From the car park head up the river valley as far as you like - Wp.6 is a good spot to turn round and retrace steps to the station. (1½ hours, 4 miles/6km)	Follow the route to Wp.9 and then turn left along the broad stony track. Leave the moor through a gate (Wp.26) to **Belstone** and continue the main route turning left at Wp.20. (2 hours, 6½ miles/10km)

Access by car: Park at **Okehampton Station** car park, on the café/station entrance side.

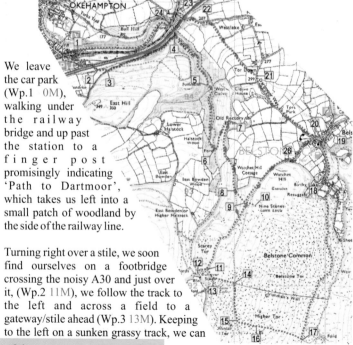

We leave the car park (Wp.1 0M), walking under the railway bridge and up past the station to a finger post promisingly indicating 'Path to Dartmoor', which takes us left into a small patch of woodland by the side of the railway line.

Turning right over a stile, we soon find ourselves on a footbridge crossing the noisy A30 and just over it, (Wp.2 11M), we follow the track to the left and across a field to a gateway/stile ahead (Wp.3 13M). Keeping to the left on a sunken grassy track, we can hear the main road alongside us as we descend towards **East Okement River**, ignoring paths uphill to the right. We soon come to the river straight ahead (Wp.4 25M) and can see the A30 flyover to our left, which we thankfully leave as we stroll off right on the **Tarka Trail** up the tranquil river valley. This is a great place for dog-walkers and it's very easy to pass the time of day here but we keep going, stepping over giant stones down by the water's edge.

The East Okement River

Crossing a small stream (Wp.5 35M) we can choose either of two gaps in the wall opposite which take us back down to the **Okement** again, which now really begins to take on some character as it carves zigzag channels through massive stone slabs, creating pools, cascades and rapids.

We climb and clamber alongside the watercourse in woodland, the scenery becoming more and more dramatic until eventually we drop down to a calmer spot with an entertaining sign inviting us to 'please close the gate' which opens straight into the river! We happily take the footbridge rather than the ford (Wp.6 48M) and walk back on ourselves for a few yards, then bear off to the right up the hill and towards the moor.

The grassy track leads us uphill for 6 minutes with the river on our left , views ahead in the distance and bracken slopes on our right, until we intersect a path and turn right, doubling back on ourselves (Wp.7 54M). We step out now, gently upwards, as the **Dartmoor** *tors* appear on the skyline ahead and broad views open up behind us. Leaving the ruined **Watchet Hill Cottage** on the left, we fork left after 5 minutes (Wp.8 65M), still going uphill and heading south-east with **Belstone Tor** ahead - but we're looking for the **Nine Stones** and so, when we meet a broad stony track (Wp.9 69M) we cross it directly, picking up a small grassy path. Keeping the *tors* and rocky outcrops to our right, the stones suddenly appear like pointy shark's teeth, especially spooky

The **Nine Stones**, the remains of a Bronze Age burial site, are also known as the **Nine Maidens**. Legend tells that they are the remains of young girls who were turned to stone as a punishment for dancing on a Sunday, and it is said that the stones come alive at midday to dance - and don't always sit down again in the same spot.

The Nine Stones

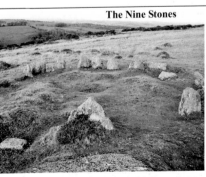

In fact, most people count sixteen or seventeen stones which probably accounts for the other name for them, the **Seventeen Brothers**.

if it's misty (Wp.10 71M).

We retrace our steps to Wp.9 and head left (SW) on the track curving round the back of **Scarey Tor** on our right, taking a right at a track junction (Wp.11 84M) towards a cluster of trees and river crossings, **Cullever Steps**, (Wp.12 86M) where two fords, two bridges and two sets of stepping stones take the traveller across the **East Okement** and **Black-a-ven Brook** near where they meet. The fascinating pavement effect of the cobbles makes for an easier crossing for horses and carts.

Our next destination is **Irishman's Wall** which we can now pick out on the slopes of **Belstone Tor**. We return to Wp.11, continue to the right and then fork left until we reach a small upright stone (Wp.13 89M) which is our marker to turn left and follow the wall straight up the hillside. After 2 minutes we join a broad track, follow it round to the right crossing the wall (Wp.14 93M) and head up to **Winter Tor**, a small rocky outcrop to the right (Wp.15 98 M). We turn left (E) uphill on not much more than a sheep track to a prominent rock on the brow (Wp.16 102M) - a good place for a picnic (assuming there's a wind-free spot) - and there's a great view all round with **Cosdon Beacon** (E), **Oke Tor** (S) and **Yes Tor** (SW). Taking the small grassy path (E) we have a clear, easy descent, with the **River Taw** meandering in the valley below, and soon come down to a stony track (Wp.17 110M).

Irishman's Wall

The story goes that in the early 19th century, two enterprising farmers hired a band of Irishmen to build a wall to enclose a large area of the moor. At that time farmers had the right to fence off 8 acres of moorland, but this project far exceeded this allowance and was viewed somewhat dimly by local landowners and farmers who saw that their access to the moor for grazing would be restricted. Accordingly a group of men from **Okehampton** and **Belstone** organized themselves to come out one night to destroy the wall – the offending farmers took the hint and the Irishmen returned home quietly.

Much of the wall still remains, running more than 1000 yards from the **Taw** over **Belstone Hill** almost down to the **East Okement**.

Turning left and stepping out briskly now, with *clitter* on our left and the river valley below on the right, we eventually approach a small settlement and we leave the moor through a metal gate (Wp.18 130M). We follow the road and soon approach the village of **Belstone** and turn right to emerge to a commemorative stone and interesting stocks on the green (Wp.19 132M, see the picture on the next page).

Our route takes us left, back towards the middle of the village (where a diversion to the pub, **The Tors**, might tempt you) and then on past the **Telegraph Office** to a right turn (Wp.20 141M).

The stocks at 138 minutes

Easy walking on the metalled road brings us to **Cleave House** on the left, and ignoring the bridle path to **West Cleave**, we keep on round, over the cattle grid to a sign to 'Fatherford' (Wp.21 152M).

Over the stile to the left, our path leads us across a field, to a gap in the hedge opposite. We follow on round to the right as directed, down the hill.

We negotiate another couple of stiles as we descend the grassy meadows until a stream faces us and we find a crossing point round to the left. Through the gate opposite (Wp.22 163M), we emerge onto a lane and curve downhill (W), under the A30 and on under the viaduct to a signpost (Wp.23 167M). We take the wide track to the left (S) and follow the **Devonshire Heartland Way** through a gate and under the viaduct arches, crossing the **East Okement** again to the right (Wp.24 170M). We are now on the home stretch as we take the bridle path to the right to **Station Road** and back under the arches yet again. A pretty stretch of woodland and a couple of gates bring us to a little stone house where we turn left up steep steps to our car and, for us anyway, a welcome cup of tea at the station (Wp.25 186M).

Our starting point is well placed for easy access to the idyllic picnic spots down by the **River Lyd** which we sample on our return. First our route takes us up to the famous **Widgery Cross** and its stunning views are matched, and even surpassed, by those we experience later from the several *tors* we visit. This is a good round trip with some fairly demanding climbs on grassy peat and then an easy tramway home - an interesting and varied walk.

Safety Advice: Please note: live firing frequently takes place on **Willsworthy Range**. It is imperative to check on the Firing Times before undertaking this walk. See the section on Dartmoor Firing Ranges in the introduction.

| 5 | 3¾ H | 10 miles/16 km | ⋀ | 420m 420m | ↻ | 3 |

Access by car:
Coming from **Okehampton** on the A386, turn left along a narrow lane just yards before the **Dartmoor Inn** and opposite the turning to **Lydford**. Continue through the gate and park in the car park.

Shortcut
Turn left (W) on the track at Wp.11 passing a boundary stone (Wp.25) rejoining the main route at Wp.23, the stepping stones over the **River Lyd** (2 ½ hrs 6 ½ miles/10 km).

We strike out through the gate on the right hand side (SE) of the car park facing the moor (Wp.1 0M).

The River Lyd (Wp.2)

Our route lies straight ahead (SE) on a grassy track with a glorious range of *tors* to our left, **Widgery Cross** standing out clearly atop of **Bray Tor**. Keeping on the main path over a couple of 'cross tracks' and heading for the gully formed by **Doctor Brook** we drop down to the **River Lyd**, finding easy stepping stones and an attractive if somewhat premature resting spot (Wp.2 10M).

The work begins as we climb **Bray Tor**, always heading for the Cross, taking a right fork at four scrubby hawthorn trees (Wp.3 12M), crossing a large track coming in at right angles after a minute. A scramble up the often indistinct path over stones and through bracken brings us to the summit and the famous landmark of **Widgery Cross** (Wp.4 32M); see the next page for a picture and background information on the cross. The views from here are superb - we can pick out **Doe Tor** (S) in the near distance and following round anticlockwise, **Hare**, **Sharp** and **Great Links Tor** all vie for our attention.

We clamber down the *clitter* at the back of the cross and bear off (SSE) towards the **Doe Tor** flagpole (and if the red flag is flying you shouldn't be up

Widgery Cross, built with massive stone blocks, forms a sturdy memorial standing thirteen feet high, erected to commemorate Queen Victoria's Golden Jubilee in 1887 and funded by William Widgery, a Devon landscape artist of renown. The Cross makes it immediately possible to identify **Bray Tor** - although, perhaps just to be different, the tor itself is known by various names; Bra, Brat, and on the latest OS maps, Bray.

here!) coming to a rectangular boundstone (Wp.5 42M).

A stretch of tumpy grass takes us (SSE) on to **Doetor Brook** in its own mini-gorge, a short diversion to the right affords a crossing point to step across to another stone (Wp.6 44M).

This block, engraved 'WD15', is one of forty-six such granite posts erected by the War Department to mark the bounds of the **Willsworthy Range**. The flagpole is straight ahead up through the bilberries, then a left turn (E) and we are at the top (Wp.7 50M) ready to admire those *tors* again.

You can just pick out another marker stone to the east below **Sharp Tor** and following the trodden track gently downhill, past a *cist* and cairn directly on our left, we soon arrive at 'WD16' (Wp.8 53M).

We bear right (SE), making a steady ascent of **Hare Tor** on a narrow path set in rough grass, making first for the dip between **Sharp** and **Hare** and then curving right and up to the summit (Wp.9 70M).

A brief respite, then we're off over the tor (E) and down the rocks on the other side towards a path we can see leading to the left (NNE) up **Rattlebrook Hill** towards **Chat Tor**, with **Sharp Tor** and **Great Links Tor** away further left.

This is great open countryside, often friendly but with the potential for considerable bleakness - our springy peat path can become boggy in winter - but undeterred we stride out, ignoring a left split to **Sharp Tor**, to the 'frowning frog' look-alike of **Chat Tor** (Wp.10 87M).

Continuing comfy walking (NNE) on this bouncy terrain down and then up again on a slight incline towards the **Higher** and **Lower Dunna Goats**, we cross an uneven area of old workings and immediately meet a well defined track coming in from the left (Wp.11 97M). We join the track heading north then after 50 yards fork left (N) climbing to **Lower Dunna Goat** (Wp.12 103M) and turn left (WNW) following a clear path - occasional boggy patches and holes in the peat challenging the knees and ankles - to **Great Links Tor** (Wp.13 115M). (Approaching **Great Links Tor** from this direction avoids further erosion of the marshy ground NE of the *tor*).

On the impressive *tor* we're soon enjoying those massive, panoramic, north to south, coast to coast views (if you're very lucky with the weather!) and the range of *tors* on show is magnificent. A trig point and peat cutter's bond-stone

Great Links Tor

can be explored and the layout of the tramway round **Woodcock Hill** is crystal clear.

From the *tor* we head back (ESE) to **Higher Dunna Goat** (Wp.14 125M) and descend crossing a track, into the **Rattle Brook** valley beyond.

The ruins of **Bleak House** (Wp.15 130M), once the residence of the manager of the **Rattlebrook** peat works, make another enticing rest spot possibly offering at least a little shelter.

We retrace our steps to the track below **Higher Dunna Goat** and turn right (N) running parallel to the brook on the right with **Hunt Tor** ahead on the skyline. Keeping to higher ground we fork left (Wp.16 135M) eventually joining the course of the old tramway running from the now derelict peat works (Wp.17 144M) with clear evidence of workings on **Amicombe Hill**; the stripes are the remains of the narrow gauge hand-pushed truck lines, stark reminders of about a hundred years of prolific activity from the middle of the 19th century.

The tramway

Turning left (W) we take the tramway initially uphill followed by an easy downhill tramp to the turning circle (Wp.18 172M). We take a sharp left (S) back on ourselves to cosy up alongside **Great Nodden**, particularly reminiscent of a whale when viewed from **Great Links**, forking right just past it (Wp.19 194M).

You'll appreciate just how kind that peat was to our feet earlier on as we cover this unforgiving stony ground, but the gentle downhill and glorious views thankfully distract us from such discomforts. At **Nodden Gate** (Wp.20 208M) we go through the wall ahead, negotiating two gates, first right then immediately left, and follow the handsome **King Wall** which used to bound the **King Way**, the main route from **Tavistock** to **Okehampton**. After two hundred yards a wooden signpost (Wp.21 210M) directs us left across a grassy field (SSE) and, guided by wooden posts, we arrive at a gate and ladder stile (Wp.22 217M). Here we take a short diversion to the left down to the river and that lovely spot promised in our introduction (Wp.23 219M).

Sheep crossing the River Lyd

Even the sheep use the stepping stones, although we actually think it's a grand place for a cooling paddle on a hot day. Retracing our steps and following the wall on our right we meander back to our car (Wp.24 228M), or perhaps refreshment at **The Dartmoor Inn**.

5 TAVY CLEAVE

Tavy Cleave is a dramatic gorge carved in granite by what is reputed to be the second fastest flowing river in Britain (the Spey in the Cairngorms has the honour of being the swiftest). The **Tavy** tumbles down 1000 feet in less than 8 miles and from it is drawn the full flowing **Mine** *leat*. We track this *leat* far into the cleave, picking up the magnificent **Tavy** as we go (calling for a bit of nimble footwork along the way) before scrambling up the side of the valley at its head. We then make for **Ger Tor** from where the views are absolutely outstanding before returning to our start point past the **Willsworthy Range** shooting butts.

Safety advice: Please note that live firing frequently takes place on **Willsworthy Range**. It is imperative to check on the Firing Times before undertaking this walk. See section on Dartmoor Firing Ranges.

Access by car: On the A386 **Tavistock** to **Okehampton** road, park one mile south of the **Dartmoor Inn** (which itself is opposite the turning to **Lydford**). The unsigned car park is clearly visible on the east of the road.

Leaving our car (Wp.1 0M) we strike out across the cattle grid on a military road into open moorland, the firing ranges quickly becoming visible to our left. After 500 yards the track splits (Wp.2 6M), and continuing on the tarmac (E), we soon come to another junction (Wp.3 9M).

Mine *leat*

Here we turn right on a gravel track (SE), cross a small *leat* and then wiggle round the concrete bunkers and parking area, heading for a footbridge over **Mine** *leat*. Training exercises often take place around here, and gun pops and smoke may arouse some interest – it's important to have checked that there's no live firing!

Across the bridge (Wp.4 14M) and turning left (E), we track the fast flowing *leat* on a grassy path, strolling past a sluice gate and over a concrete walkway.

As **Willsworthy Brook** drops down (Wp.5 29M) we follow the leat curving to the right and take a short diversion along a wire fence, climbing over wooden slats in the corner to rejoin the water. A boundary wall comes down on the left with **Ger Tor** just beyond it, the massive bulk of **Standon Down** facing us; red and white poles indicate that we are still within Range boundaries.

Leats are interesting and useful waterways. **Mine** leat (also known as **Wheal Friendship**) is one of those which can trick the eye by appearing to flow uphill as the terrain and river-flow slip away from it. The *leat*, which takes a considerable volume of water from the **Tavy** at its headweir, was used to supply power to the water wheels of **Wheal Friendship** copper mine at **Mary Tavy** in the 1800s. The water now finds its way (along with **Wheal Jewell** *leat*) to **Wheal Jewell** reservoir, all 6½ million gallons worth, which provides an impressive operating head of 500 feet for the **Mary Tavy** hydro-electric power station.

Our path takes us below **Nat Tor** (Wp.6 50M) and as the leat swings north we get our first glimpse up the cleave with **Ger Tor** rearing up above us.

We walk on heading ever deeper into the cleave, the leat gliding on our left and the **River Tavy** rushing past to our right. Soon we catch sight of the *leat* headweir (Wp.7 61M) and make our way across the water on a concrete ledge around the side of the small cube-shaped building.

Now the terrain becomes more challenging as we follow the river; the path narrows and we clamber over rocks to avoid boggy patches – but the water always entertains us as it dashes and falls on our right.

The River Tavy

All this hard work eventually brings us to the confluence of the **Tavy** with **Rattle Brook** and a pleasant picnic spot on the bend of the river (Wp.8 95M).

Keeping round to the left (N) we follow the brook for 100 yards, still negotiating rocks and bogs and then head off north-west, zigzagging up the slopes of **Hare Tor** over rough grass and heather. This is quite steep at first but we soon hit a grassy track (Wp.9 105M) and turn left (SW) on it, contouring around the hill below the summit. The rocky outcrops of **Tavy Cleave Tors** attract us as we step out towards them, **Hare Tor** rising on our right and **Ger Tor** coming into view ahead. At the third crag (Wp.10 116M) we pick up a grassy path towards **Ger Tor**, heading west initially to the ridge linking **Ger** and **Hare Tors**, going straight on at a gully (Wp.11 120M), always towards the top of **Ger Tor**.

The door jambs at Wp.12

Our path takes us right alongside a Bronze Age settlement – the impressive door jambs to a stone hut are easily spotted (Wp.12 125M) and further remains are abundant further up the slope. Keeping straight on (SW) we soon reach the summit of **Ger Tor** (Wp.13 133M) - and the views are superb! **Fur Tor** dominates the skyline to the east, the river tumbles down the cleave and **Hare**, **Sharp** and **Doe Tors** lead the eye north and round to **Widgery Cross** on top of **Bray Tor**. The beautiful countryside of Devon with Cornwall beyond lies to the west before we turn to **Standon Down** to the south bringing us at last full circle – breathtaking!

We set off just west of north, on a faint track towards the left of **Widgery Cross** in the distance and soon spy a boundary wall coming up the hill (the other end of which we saw earlier). We head to the top of it over tumpy grass, using sheep tracks to make life easier where possible and, as we meet it (Wp.14 142M), follow it (NW), stepping out in the direction of **Widgery Cross**. We step through a gap in the now mossy, grassy wall, skirt a small enclosed reservoir avoiding a boggy area and still follow the wall. It appears as a dark scar on the grass as it curves away to the west and it is a useful guide. Two tracks become one as we join a route descending from **Hare Tor** (Wp.15 159M), and we keep straight on with our wall, keeping to the left as we meet a broad, stony military track coming from **Wallabrook Head** (Wp.16 162M).

This is easy walking now, and we stride out past the firing range targets, past the pillars marking target distance and onto tarmac back to the car park (Wp.17 187M).

6 PETER TAVY & THE LANGSTONE

To get a feel for wild, open, remote Dartmoor with fabulous views, this expedition must be a strong contender amongst the walks on offer. But this one has the added interest of a return trek past a gorgeous river picnic spot, a beautiful *leat* in shaded woodland and finally a 'steeplechase' home to keep you limbered up! And the two good pubs en route will offer welcome salvation and comfort just when it's needed.

Please note: live firing frequently takes place on **Merrivale Range**. It is imperative to check on the Firing Times before undertaking this walk. See section on Dartmoor Firing Ranges.

Access by car: from the A386 **Tavistock** to **Okehampton** road take the turning towards **Peter Tavy**. One mile after **Harford Bridge** and just past the church in **Peter Tavy**, turn right on a narrow 'no through' lane. Park on the left after ½ mile in the quarry remains car park.

Stephens Grave

The story goes that in the 18th century a certain John Stephens was disappointed in love and sadly committed suicide - a sin back in those times. The custom then was to bury the body far from habitation and preferably at a cross-roads or parish boundary in order to confuse the Devil and any wandering evil spirits. The stone has recently been reset and the letter 'S' marked on the base for all to see.

After leaving the car park (Wp.1 0M) and turning left on the lane, we come to a sign to 'Stephens Grave and White Tor' (Wp.2 1M) and turn left along a broad gravel track. Always keeping to the main path, we climb **Smeardon Down** (NE) and as our route levels out between stone walls we arrive at the open moor with its typical sheep-cropped grassy terrain. The crags of **White Tor** ahead (with the circular pound on its south-west slopes just visible) are tempting, but first we stop at **Stephens Grave** sited a couple of yards to the right of our path (Wp.3 21M).

Continuing (NE) on our track, there's a choice after 400 yards (Wp.4 26M) - you can fork right straight to the **Langstone** and Wp.6 or, as we prefer, you can follow the track to the left climbing **White Tor**. Passing a turning circle, we clamber up the rocky tor with its military flagpole (Wp.5 36M), and relish far-reaching views to the coast and moorland. In the near distance (E) you can pick out the solitary **Langstone**, and we set off for it past an army watch post on the left, across short grass and rocks and then over tracts of grassy 'molehills' making a bumpy passage into the firing range.

Great Mis looms to our right and as we near the stone, a great swing of hills appears on the left - quite a setting for this impressive monument (Wp.6 48M).

A number of tracks leave the stone and we select a grass path (NE) on a gentle uphill towards a struggling tree in a wall ahead and cut across to it (Wp.7 57M). A wire fence comes up from the left to join a stone wall at the corner, which we follow on our left (NE) on an intermittent track uphill. As we level out at the next corner (Wp.8 68M) we leave the wall, keeping on the track towards the marshy head of **Youldon Brook**.

After six minutes we turn sharp left at a crossing point to head across rough ground down to the stream (Wp.9 75M). Fording it, we strike out (NW) on rough grass towards the corner of the wall ahead (Wp.10 83M), then carry straight on beside the wall. It's uneven walking over wettish grass and peat, but with lovely views of **Lynch Tor** to the right and the massive bulk of **Standon Down** to its left, eventually reaching a corridor where we keep to the wall on the right, then head off the moor at a gate (Wp.11 92M).

The Langstone

Set in this lonely spot on the moor, this famous standing stone is in fact the terminal *menhir* for a scarcely visible stone row. Originating in the Bronze Age, it survives to this day and has probably been used as a waymark for workers and travellers over the centuries. A more recent use has been as target practice - the holes made by those firing can be clearly seen on the eastern side.

Strolling along the stony track past the low crags of **Bagga Tor** on the right, we turn left through a gate as our track becomes a pleasant country lane (Wp.12 99M) offering us lovely views ahead. After half a mile, at an

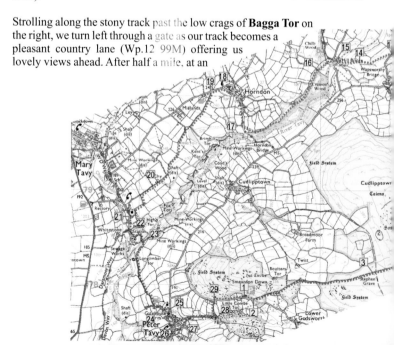

easily missable signpost on the right where the road curves to the left (Wp.13 111M), we make our way over steep steps in the wall - not easy to negotiate! The path heads diagonally (SW) for a gate in a wall and through it, we make for a gap in the next wall ahead (Wp.14 117M) and bearing right, keep to the wall down to **Hill Bridge**.

Hill Bridge

A little stile takes us onto the bridge and across it; we forgo the unappealing metal ladder down to the river and instead take wooden steps further on the left to this delightful resting place (Wp.15 121M). If there's still food in the backpack, now's the time to sit back and enjoy it whilst surveying the flood openings along the bridge, designed to cater for the impetuous **Tavy**, the river itself with its salmon ladder and the gentle *leat* alongside.

The *leat*

With the *leat* headweir on our right and the river on our left, we set off on the narrow concrete left bank on a delightful stretch through pretty woodland, accompanied by the stream.

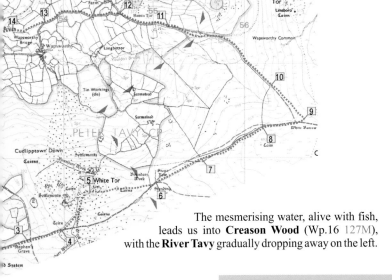

The mesmerising water, alive with fish, leads us into **Creason Wood** (Wp.16 127M), with the **River Tavy** gradually dropping away on the left.

Woodland turns to pasture and after a couple of stiles the *leat* enters a short tunnel and we face a path at right angles (Wp.17 143M) where we turn right towards **Horndon**, puffing up the narrow gravel track. As we meet a lane we continue straight on, then fork left in **Horndon** and turn left again towards **Mary Tavy** at the next junction (Wp.18 152M).

The chimney at Wp.20

After 100 yards we take the wide, signposted track to the left (Wp.19 153M), unless of course you wish to divert down the lane for a further 100 yards to **The Elephant's Nest** - a most attractive 16th century inn. Yellow waymarks now lead us on our 'steeplechase' to the church at **Mary Tavy** - there are three gates and six substantial stiles to negotiate on our way down across a series of fields - stiles can start to lose their charm….. The path is clear, generally heading south-west and, ignoring other routes to the right, we pass a derelict chimney (Wp.20 177M) to come down to **Mary Tavy** church (Wp.21 186M).

We turn left along the lane, continuing straight ahead by the entrance to **Mary Tavy** power station (actually water works) (Wp.22 189M) on the blue waymarked track to **Peter Tavy**, downhill and amongst trees. Through a gate, we are with the **Tavy** again, a well placed bench on the right and a wooden footbridge across the water (Wp.23 192M). We set off over and up, around to the right on the bridlepath and then contour above the river before climbing to what's now a tarmac lane to **The Peter Tavy Inn** (Wp.24 204M). Strolling to the left past the church and village cross (Wp.25 206M), we drop to the 'main' road in **Peter Tavy** and turn right for 100 yards to the village hall (Wp.26 208M). We turn left on a path with a pretty stream tumbling down beside us past the Methodist Church.

Emerging to a small lane, we cross the bridge to the left (Wp.27 210M) and continue with a steep little section on tarmac before the road narrows to a track between high hedges. Through a metal gate, we come to a wooden signpost in trees (Wp.28 216M) and turn sharp left to a little green gate labelled 'bridlepath', the tunnel-like track leading us up alongside a cottage. The path broadens and we're out onto moorland through another gate; straight ahead is the road (Wp.29 221M) and, still relentlessly uphill, we turn right and march back to our car (Wp.30 226M).

7 GREAT MIS & GREAT STAPLE TORS

Great Mis and **Great Staple** tors are the highest peaks in this part of Dartmoor which afford stunning views down to the South Devon coast. This fine weather walk first takes in **Great Mis Tor** then heads into the upper **Walkham Valley**, visiting an ancient stone circle and settlement before returning along the impressive **Roos Tor** to **Great Staple Tor** ridge. We return via the derelict **Merrivale Quarry** and a possible refreshment stop at **The Dartmoor Inn**, followed by a stroll along the fascinating **Merrivale** stone rows.

Please note: live firing frequently takes place on **Merrivale Range**. It is imperative to check on the Firing Times before undertaking this walk. See section on Dartmoor Firing Ranges.

4 | 3H | 7½ miles/12 km | 370m / 370m | 2

Access by car: On the B3357 **Tavistock** to **Princetown** road, park one mile east of **The Dartmoor Inn** at **Merrivale** on the south side of the road.

Great Mis Tor

Leaving the car park (Wp.1 0M), we cross the road to the side of a red metal barrier and take the stony track (N). The mast at **North Hessary Tor** rises on the right, **Great Staple** and **Roos Tor** dominate the ridge on our left, but **Little Mis Tor** ahead is our first destination (Wp.2 19M). Looking back, the views to the south open up down the **River Tamar Valley**, past the **Tamar Bridge** and out to **Plymouth Sound**, while we continue on a grassy track, still north towards the rocks and flag pole of **Great Mis Tor**. The track forks (Wp.3 22M) and we keep left heading for the summit passing a boundary stone (Wp.4 26M) just before the final climb to the top of the massive granite crags and the impressive all round views (Wp.5 30M).

Continuing north we pass another smaller outcrop topped by the small rock basin known as **Mistor Pan**, then head for a square MOD building (Wp.6 35M). Passing the hut, we stay on the same course over *clitter* and then grass as we drop down into a small valley and turn left (WNW), half a minute after passing the lowest point along the north of the valley (Wp.7 43M). We meet the **River Walkham** as it rushes below from a steep sided cutting (Wp.8 50M) and turn right upstream, climbing and contouring round the steep river bank. Following round to the right, the ground levels and we find opportunities to cross as the valley heads round to the east (Wp.9 65M). Note: crossing maybe difficult after heavy rain.

Over the river, we head north up **Dead Lake Valley** (Wp.10 72M), littered with old tin mine workings, before a track crosses our path (Wp.11 78M) where we turn left, paddling through a shallow ford then on an indistinct grassy path. We climb gently, following the line of the river valley below (SW) to the brow of the rounded hill.

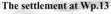

The settlement at Wp.13

Just as the ground starts to fall away, we find **Langstone Moor** stone circle, sadly damaged by the US Army during WWII, only seven stones now remaining upright (Wp.12 93M). From here we head downhill (S) and after 250 yards on the closely grazed hillside, we discover a collection of hut circles scattered around the south facing slope; a well-chosen spot for a settlement! (Wp.13 96M)

Our route now takes us southwest, still following the line of the valley, directly to **Roos Tor** along sheep tracks. The river and **Grimstone Leat** are clearly visible in the valley to our left. As we approach the tor, silhouetted against the sky like an old battleship, we climb steadily passing a stone pillar, 'B' carved on its side signifying the land of the Duke of Bedford.

Roos Tor Logan stone

Up on the tor, we find an impressive Logan stone and great views (Wp.14 120M). Straight over the tor, we follow the well-trodden path past another bound stone towards the biggest granite tower of **Great Staple Tor** (Wp.15 128M) with its stunning views down the **Tamar Valley** to **Plymouth**.

Merrivale Quarry

The path continues clearly down from **Great Staple Tor** across rock-strewn ground to **Middle Staple Tor** (Wp.16 133M), from where we look down to **Vixen Tor**, **Merrivale** and **King's Tor** beyond. Leaving the tor (SE), we head in the direction of the television mast on a rough track through heather and gorse. As we drop down, the fencing around the edge of **Merrivale Quarry** is visible and we head for the corner (Wp.17 142M) to peer over into the derelict flooded working below.

Turning right along the fence, we make our way down to the road (Wp.18 147M), cross it and turn left. A grass verge makes for easy walking as we head down into the sharp **Merrivale** dip, stopping for refreshments at **The Dartmoor Inn** if required before crossing the bridge over the **River Walkham** and climbing out of the valley.

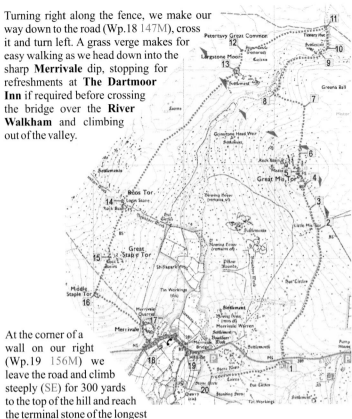

At the corner of a wall on our right (Wp.19 156M) we leave the road and climb steeply (SE) for 300 yards to the top of the hill and reach the terminal stone of the longest of the **Merrivale** stone rows (Wp.20 162M). It's worth investigating this famous site and further information is included with Walk 27. Following the row leads us directly back to the wall and trees surrounding the carpark (Wp.21 173M).

8 BEARDOWN MAN & WISTMAN'S WOOD

The views from **Beardown Tors** are stunning and this walk takes us gently up there alongside a *leat* with just a short (but quite steep) climb to the top. But from there we strike out across wild terrain in remote Dartmoor country to meet up with **Beardown Man** at **Devil's Tor** before gradually dropping down again, passing the fascinating trees of **Wistman's Wood** on our way.

Please note: live firing frequently takes place on **Merrivale Range**. It is imperative to check on the Firing Times before undertaking this walk. See section on Dartmoor Firing Ranges.

Access by car: At **Two Bridges** on the B3357 **Tavistock** to **Dartmeet** road, park in the car park directly opposite the **Two Bridges Hotel**.

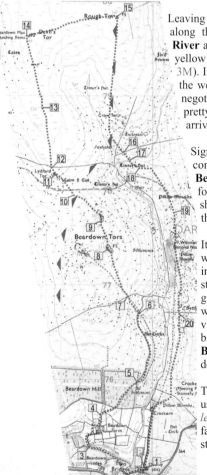

Leaving the car (Wp.1 0M), we turn right along the road crossing the **West Dart River** and right again after 200 yards at a yellow waymarked public footpath (Wp.2 3M). Immediately over a stile, we follow the well-trodden path gently uphill and, negotiating another three stiles with the pretty **Cowsic River** on our right, we arrive at a bridge (Wp.3 12M).

Signs direct us right across the water to continue on the main track past **Beardown Farm** to a *leat* which we follow right (Wp.4 18M), passing a sheep *leap* after 1 minute (rather them than me!).

It's easy walking alongside the water, first across open fields then into conifers, which we exit over a stile (Wp.5 26M). We now have a good stretch out alongside the watercourse with **Wistman's Wood** visible across the valley on the right below **Longaford Tor**, and **Beardown Tors** ahead, the flagpole denoting the firing range.

The narrow grassy/rocky path brings us to a simple stone bridge across the *leat* (Wp.6 39M); we turn left on a faint track onto the moor heading steeply (NNW) up the hill. Bearing away from the brow as we climb, we come to a yellow waymarked gate in a stone wall (Wp.7 44M) and continue straight on, making for the flagpole on the tor ahead (Wp.8 53M). The views are superb - you can pick out H.M. Prison at **Princetown** (SSW) near the mast at **North Hessary Tor**, **Great Mis** (W) and **Wistman's Wood** (E) in the foreground, with **Bellever** and **Haytor** way off in the distance.

The ladder stile at Wp.12

A diversion west to explore the other crags is a possibility but we continue (NNW) across and over a smaller tor (Wp.9 58M) from where we head straight towards **Lydford Tor** (NW) on open moorland with wet patches, lumpy grass and occasional heather. Using sheep tracks to ease our way, we cross into the range, meeting the **Lich Way** head on (Wp.10 65M).

We maintain our bearing (NW) striking out for **Lydford Tor** (Wp.11 71M) then make for the very obvious ladder stile in the wall ahead - a useful landmark (Wp.12 73M).

Beardown Man

In search of **Beardown Man**, the going's quite tough on a grassy track to the bald hill ahead, where gaiters and a stick might come in handy as wet patches and tufty grass impede our progress.

Avoiding a pool on our left (Wp.13 83M), we begin the gentle ascent past a small tor to drier ground and the modest **Devil's Tor** - but standing beside it is the most impressive **Beardown Man** (Wp.14 96M). At this remote spot, the eleven-foot high *menhir* is completely isolated - none of the usual stone rows or circles accompanying it.

From the low rise of **Devil's Tor** the square MOD buildings on **Rough Tor** are visible (E); we set off using sheep tracks over peaty, mossy, grassy, (wet!) ground for a 15 minute demanding hike. The open moor around this tor is wild and desolate (Wp.15 112M), though there's a bit of shelter by the rocks and you're quite likely to be joined by some ponies also seeking dry ground.

It's pretty much a steady downhill return now, starting with a wander over springy terrain following the line of the range poles (S) and past **Crow Tor** to cross a ladder stile in a stone wall (Wp.16 134M), carrying straight on towards a 'stream' - the juvenile **West Dart River** (Wp.17 137M).

Big boulders help us across, which can be tricky after rain, and we head uphill, bearing left after ½ minute on a track towards **Longaford Tor**. We meet a bigger track (Wp.18 141M) and contour (left then right) below the rocky outcrop, with lovely views of the river valley, to the northern end of **Wistman's Wood** (Wp.19 152M).

Wistman's Wood

Famous for its abundance of rare upland oak, those wonderfully twisted, stunted and gnarled trees, with their blankets of also important moss, fern and lichen, the trees of **Wistman's Wood** are indeed ancient. In 1620 the trees were "no taller than a man may touch the top with his head".

They've grown a bit over the years though, their average height today being about six metres.

Crocken Tor

Crocken Tor (SSW) from where we stand at Wp.20) was from at least the 15thC the seat of the Stannary Parliament where representatives from the districts of **Tavistock, Chagford, Ashburton** and **Plympton** would meet to discuss and order their affairs. As tin mining became less profitable so the Parliament became less relevant, fading by the mid 18th century.

Keeping in line with the edge of the wood to preserve this fragile environment (with any dogs firmly under control), we continue (S) on a clear path parallel to the river past these fascinating trees to a stile (Wp.20 167M) which takes us out to **Crocken Tor** *Newtake*.

Our well-worn track is still straight ahead and takes us round the back of **Crockern** cottage from where we take the broad gravel driveway to return to our car (Wp.21 190M).

This walk combines a stroll through **Fernworthy Forest** with an excursion on to the open moor, visiting ancient stone circles and rows and the impressive **East Dart River** valley as it carves its way around the tors. It is a splendid walk for a summer's day providing good views, sheltered picnic spots and shade in the forest.

4 | 3½ H | 9½ miles/15 km | 250m / 250m | ↻ 0 | 🍴🍽

Access by car:
Head down **Chagford High Street** away from the church and fork left into **Manor Road**. At **Waye Barton** keep round to the left and ¾ mile further on at **Tunnaford** fork right, following the sign to **Fernworthy Reservoir**. Ignore a left turn and keep straight on at **Shapley Cross** still following the signs. Cross a cattle grid on to the moor and continue past the **Fernworthy** carpark on the right following the road to its end on the western side of reservoir and park.

From the parking area (Wp.1 0M) we go through a gate and take a footpath signed 'To the moor' following a broad forestry track (W) between the conifers. After 150 yards we fork left as the track splits, reaching **Fernworthy Circle** and stone row 300 yards further on on the right (Wp.2 7M). We continue straight on, gently climbing (WNW) to the top of the hill and crossing two tracks. As we start to descend our path narrows and after crossing another track we reach the edge of the forest and a gate onto the rolling moor (Wp.3 26M), with the ruin of **Teignhead Farm** to the west and **Sittaford Tor** south-west, which we head for.

GREY WETHERS

The Bronze Age **Grey Wethers** site is unique on **Dartmoor** in having two stone circles almost identical in diameter sited next to one another on a north-south line. The circles were excavated in 1898 and restored in 1909. As with many of Dartmoor's features the site has stories associated with it and one such story tells of a farmer who had recently moved to Dartmoor who stopped for a drink at **Warren House Inn**, and helped by several pints of scrumpy, was persuaded by the locals that there was an excellent flock of high quality sheep nearby which he would be welcome to buy. They walked off in search of them, and through the mist the farmer saw what he took to be a fine flock. He agreed to the sale, and returned to the site the following morning to find that what he'd taken to be sheep were actually the stones of **Grey Wethers**!

Our narrow well-trodden path descends gradually towards the shallow valley on our right, passing between two old stone gateposts (Wp.4 32M) and altering course (S), we make for the saddle to the left of **Sittaford Tor** and a gate (Wp.5 44M) in a wall visible on the skyline ahead. Through the gate, we continue south and after 200 yards arrive at **Grey Wethers** double stone circle (Wp.6 45M)

Leaving the stones we turn towards **Sittaford Tor** (W), following a distinct path running parallel to the wall on our right. As we climb, we can see the regular shape of the **Grey Wethers** monument below and behind us more clearly. Arriving at **Sittaford Tor** (Wp.7 55M), although not very high, we are rewarded with wild views of the moor around us. Our next destination is **Statts House** on **Winney's Down** on the same heading (SW) as the wall we have just followed.

We climb a ladder stile and continue with the wall for 20 yards; then as it splits right and left, we strike out on a little-used path in the middle across coarse grass. As we drop down into a shallow valley the ground becomes wet and we must pick our way through, stepping on clumps of grass to find the remains of **Statts House** (Wp.8 74M), a ruined 19th century peat cutters' shelter - although it provides little shelter in its present state, it does at least offer a place to sit and enjoy the excellent views.

The waterfall at Wp.10

Legs rested, we set off (S) downhill on a clear path towards **East Dart River** which cuts its way across the moor at right angles to us. As we reach the water (Wp.9 84M) we bear left, following it downstream as it meanders through **Sandy Hole Pass**, a sheltered and tranquil area, then continue on the left bank, following in the footsteps of many others.

Just after passing old tin mining spoils the river dramatically dives over a waterfall (Wp.10 102M); we follow it as it continues to tumble down the valley which bears round left (E) and becomes increasingly gorge-like.

Where two large rocks stick out of a small grassy island in the river (Wp.11 106M) we turn left, diverging from the river. Our narrow path climbs gradually and contours round the gorge with the river below on our right, then starts to descend, passing through a gate in a wall (Wp.12 121M) back down to river level, following it as it curves round to the right. Just after the apex of the bend, we turn sharply left back on ourselves up a side tributary to look for

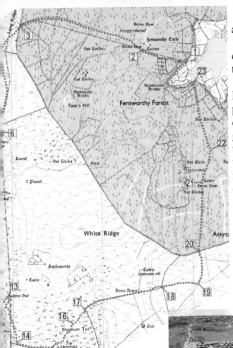

an ancient *Beehive Hut* (Wp.13 128M) which we find on the opposite bank, 200 yards from the main river.

Returning to the **East Dart**, we pick up the riverside path downstream to a stone wall and gate which we do not go through (Wp.14 137M), turning left instead (E) on a narrow track uphill with a wall on our right, soon catching sight of the impressive structure known as the **Scotch Sheepfold** (Wp.15 143M), built in the 19th century as a factory for extracting starch from locally grown potatoes and later converted into a sheepfold.

Scotch Sheepfold

From this remarkable building with its substantial vertical stones set in its walls, we set off (NE) climbing steeply up **Stannon Tor** following sheep tracks through the gorse and *clitter* to the summit (Wp.16 151M).

From there we can clearly see **Fernworthy Forest** ahead and we continue (NE) across tumpy grass down to the corner of a stone boundary wall (Wp.17 155M) where we head east, following the wall on our right as it drops into a pronounced valley. Climbing out of the dip, we follow the wall-side until it ends (Wp.18 169M) where we negotiate a stile on our right immediately followed by a second on our left. We continue on our grassy path (E) parallel to but 300 yards from the edge of **Fernworthy** until we come to a cross tracks (Wp.19 176M) at which we turn left (N), making for a gate leading into the plantation (Wp.20 182M) where we go straight ahead on a broad forestry track through the conifers.

After 900 yards, a small clearing on the left of the track (Wp.21 190M) reveals the Assycombe stone row in a magical setting, one of the best we've seen, marching down hill with terminal stones at both ends and a *cist* at the top.

We continue on the broad track turning left at a T-junction (Wp.22 194M) and straight on at a couple of cross tracks before joining the road (Wp.23 205M) and turning left back to the parking area (Wp.24 213M).

10 POSTBRIDGE: EXPLORING THE EAST DART

This walk explores the enchanting **East Dart** valley, zigzagging across the river over interesting bridges or bold stepping stones. Wildlife accompanies us as we meander along the beautiful river banks, savouring the tranquil surroundings. We return through the ancient settlements of **Babeny** and **Pizwell**, enjoying typical Dartmoor farming scenery. It's a walk suitable for all weathers, as we don't venture on to the high moor.

3 | 3H 20M | 9½ miles/15 km | 200m / 200m | 3

Access by car: Park in the car park at **Postbridge** on the B3212 **Princetown** to **Moretonhampstead** road.

Extension
This walk can be extended by combining it at waypoint 14 with walk 36 (Dartmeet).

From the carpark (Wp.1 0M) we turn left, passing the Post Office and shop, then crossing over the main road to walk down towards the **East Dart** river. Before reaching the bridge we take a footpath through a gate on the right signed 'Bellever' (Wp.2 2M), passing on our left the famous **Postbridge Clapper Bridge**.

Our path winds its way up steps through gorse bushes before emerging onto open common land, then gradually converges with the lane to **Bellever** on the right, flanked by the trees of the **Bellever** plantation (Wp.3 16M). We continue along the lane downhill into the village; cottages and a grey phone box on the left.

Bellever clapper bridge

Where the road bends right we carry straight on through a small gate (Wp.4 25M) along a little track through gorse, cutting off the corner. Meeting the road again (Wp.5 27M), we turn left and stroll down crossing the **Bellever** road bridge (Wp.6 31M) alongside the ancient clapper bridge which sadly lost its central span during floods.

Over the bridge, we turn right to follow one of the many well-trodden tracks along the riverside with the dark interior of **Bellever** forest occupying the other bank. We come to an old wall marking the end of permitted land (Wp.7 45M) and turn left, having a thankfully short but steep scramble up the valley side, keeping the wall on our right.

At the wall's corner (Wp.8 49M) we turn right, going round the private enclosure to reach its end (Wp.9 58M) where we descend to the river at the impressive **Laughter Hole Stepping Stones** (Wp.10 62M).

Trying to appear confident while striding across the stones (children never seem to have a problem with this), we turn left along a track on the other side, through a gate, then left over a ladder stile onto a path heading south. We climb steadily up the valley side, pushing our way through thick gorse to reach a boundary wall (Wp.11 74M) and turn left along a well-used path parallel with the river in the valley below.

Crossing an old wall (Wp.12 78M), we head down towards the river across a well-grazed field, then make our way along the bank, diverting inland as we come to a small hillock. We now need to negotiate a short stretch of very wet bog (climbing up and round seems to be the best solution) before continuing along the river to a stile taking us into the woods of **Little Newtake Plantation** (Wp.13 94M), where we turn left.

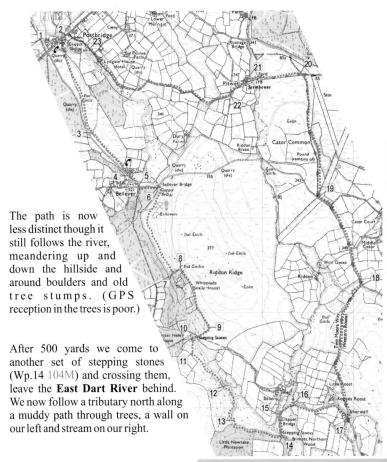

The path is now less distinct though it still follows the river, meandering up and down the hillside and around boulders and old tree stumps. (GPS reception in the trees is poor.)

After 500 yards we come to another set of stepping stones (Wp.14 104M) and crossing them, leave the **East Dart River** behind. We now follow a tributary north along a muddy path through trees, a wall on our left and stream on our right.

A small clapper bridge allows us to cross the stream (Wp.15 108M) which we follow on our left as it cuts its way across charming open pasture up to an unfenced lane leading to **Babeny** (Wp.16 111M), where we turn right. Wandering up out of the small valley on this peaceful lane, we pass **Rogues Roost** on our left then **Sherwell Farm** on our right, turning left just after the farm house (Wp.17 121M) on our footpath to **Cator Gate**.

> ### Babeny and Pizwell
> A number of old farmsteads known as Ancient Tenements, such as **Babeny** and **Pizwell,** were granted grazing rights on Dartmoor . These originate back to the mid 13th century, when the region referred to as the 'Forest of Dartmoor' was an area predominantly reserved for the Kings of England (and later, for the Duchy of Cornwall) for hunting deer and other game.

The rough path turns sharp left, climbing between gorse bushes on to the moor, then levelling out and following a boundary wall on our left before striking out north. The farm track down to **Riddon Farm** appears on our left but we continue parallel with it until we reach a road and turn left (Wp.18 142M). Now we can stretch our legs along this quiet, undulating lane flanked by verdant stone walls, fields either side. A magnificent avenue of old beech trees (planted as a wind break) crosses the road, and immediately after it (Wp.19 155M) we turn right through a small wooden gate onto a blue way marked bridlepath. We head north on an indistinct path across **Cator Common**, making for the conifers of **Soussons Wood** ahead. Before reaching the trees we pass through a gate (Wp.20 173M) and leave the bridlepath, turning left on a stony track towards **Pizwell** which drops down through heather and gorse to a ford and half-submerged stepping stones – very cooling for the feet!

The ancient settlement of Pizwell

The ancient settlement of **Pizwell** is just ahead (Wp.21 181M), and our path signed 'Lydgate and Postbridge' takes us straight on and then left, skirting round the back of the farm. We pass through a wooden gate and bear right, following the track alongside a wall on the left, unfenced on the right.

A few yards past a metal gate, the track splits (Wp.22 185M), and we turn right to **Postbridge**, dropping down to a ford before climbing again between gorse hedges. The clearly marked track heads west, then drops down towards the **East Dart River**, swinging right and parallel with the river towards **Lydgate House**. Through a small wooden gate alongside the house, we turn left along the hotel drive. After 150 yards we take a small kissing gate left (Wp.23 210M) onto a permitted path to the **Postbridge Clapper Bridge**, making our way across muddy ground alongside the river to cross the majestic bridge and then turn left on the main road back to the car (Wp.24. 219M).

Refreshments are available at **Postbridge** Post Office and at the two hotels.

11 BENNETT'S CROSS - CHALLACOMBE - GOLDEN DAGGER MINE

This area of Dartmoor is steeped in history, with abundant evidence of settlements extending back to the Bronze Age. Mining is the most recent activity here and this walk takes us through some of the deserted workings of **Golden Dagger** and **Vitifer**, past **Challacombe** medieval village, and also takes in the renowned **Warren House Inn** with its famous open fire.

3 | 2½ H | 7 miles/11 km | 200m / 200m | 3

Access by car:
Take the B 3212 **Moretonhampstead** to **Princetown** road. Just before the **Warren House Inn**, park in small car park on the left, adjacent to the roadside stone cross.

There are two optional starts; either a brisk climb up and over **Birch Tor**, or a less energetic descent to **Vitifier Mine** and a gentle climb over the saddle to **Headland Warren Farm**.

Option (a)
We start at the car park (Wp.1 0M) adjacent to the ancient boundary marker of **Bennett's Cross** and take the **Two Moors Way** (E) following a well worn peaty track up **Birch Tor**. From the top (Wp.2 13M) we enjoy good views of the surrounding moor, with **Nattadon** and **Meldon** hills (N), **Fernworthy Forest** (W), the forests of **Soussons** and **Bellever** (S) and the tors of **Hookney**, **King** and **Hameldown** (E). We stay on the **Two Moors Way** until a fork (Wp.3 20M) where we bear right and meet a road (Wp.4 24M). Here we turn right; not on the road, but on a small grassy track running downhill between heathers, passing a circular enclosure on the left, heading for **Headland Warren Farm** which nestles at the head of the valley, sheltered by trees. Just before the farm we cross a bridle path signed 'Warren House Inn' right and 'Grimspound' left (Wp.5 32M). It's here that we rejoin with Option **(b)** heading straight on.

Option (b)
Starting at the **Bennett's Cross** car park (Wp.1 0M) we pass the ancient boundary marker and head south-east on a grassy track down into the valley among the old **Vitifer Mine** workings. A small stream joins us on the left, crosses our path and then disappears underground only to reappear from the ground 20 yards further on. We join a track and head left, still following the stream. About 200 yards further on we come to a level grassy area with the remains of the mine buildings clearly visible (Wp.15 15M). From here we continue heading south with the stream on our right, bearing left (E) after 25 yards to climb gently alongside a boundary wall. We follow the old mine workings up and over a saddle between **Birch Tor** and **Challacombe Down** hill, noticing

Bennett's Cross

a fine prehistoric triple stone row on the right with **Headland Warren Farm** visible in the valley below. We follow the path down until we reach a signpost (Wp.5 36M) where we join Option **(a)** turning right.

We head towards **Challacombe** (SE) through a small gate at the side of the farmhouse following a stream and stone wall on the right and past the farm on the left. After about 200 yards, by a nissen-type corrugated barn, our track forks right through a gate with a blue waymark, down into the valley.

Headland Warren Farm dates back at least 600 years and is believed to have been a Dartmoor longhouse. These rectangular buildings were usually built into the side of a hill and housed both people and animals under the same roof – animals at the lower end. In the mid 18thC it became 'Warren Farm' and in the 1830s was used as a hostelry serving local miners.

Challacombe Medieval Village

The well-trodden path now heads along the valley (S) between **Hamel Down** and **Challacombe Down**, with the scarring of mine workings on the right-hand hillside, and spoil heaps by the river on the left. We arrive at **Challacombe Cottages** (Wp.6 50M) via a gate (blue dot on post), then pass through another gate and carry straight on along a concrete road to the site of **Challacombe Medieval Village** on our right. (Wp.7 52M). Well worth exploring!

Continuing in front of a farmhouse on our right, we go through a gate and along a muddy bridle path, climbing gently from a small pond and stream on our left to a fork in the path (Wp.8 59M). We bear left on the bridle path to **Soussons**, initially climbing and swinging to the right, then dropping gradually across rough pasture towards a stream in the valley ahead, now heading west towards **Soussons** plantation, its mature conifers dominating the skyline in front of us. We cross a stile – dogs are provided for nicely here – and follow the path over the stream and up the muddy bank to a gate at the top of the rise (Wp.9 70M). Through this, we swing round to the left, following the fence (S) towards **Soussons Farm** then, still in the field, we cross a stream to a gate in the south-west corner (Wp.10 78M). At the crossroads we take the bridle path sharp right signed to 'Bennett's Cross' on a grassy track alongside the plantation (NNW), then through a gate into the wood (Wp.11 84M). Climbing gently, our waymarked path heads north through the trees, crosses a forestry road, and then descends gradually to join another gravel road (Wp.12. 92M). Here, we bear left for 200 yards, then fork right back onto the waymarked path.

Our path crosses a stream and converges with a wide, distinct track (Wp.13 97M). **Bennett's Cross** and our car is to the left but it's worth a quick 15 minute diversion 500 yards to the right, to the interesting ruins of the **Golden Dagger Tin Mine** (Wp.14 101M).

Returning to Wp.13, we stay on the wide track (N) towards **Bennett's Cross**, passing through marshy land, low willow bushes and plenty of evidence of past mining activity, eventually arriving at an open grassy clearing marking the site of the **Birch Tor** and **Vitifer** mine. (Wp.15 125M). This is a favourite picnic spot for many in summer, with its fast flowing stream, sheltered location and mysterious past.

Mining Gerts

It would be difficult not to notice the deep scars or *gerts* on the hillsides all around this part of Dartmoor, proof of the area's long association with tin mining extending back over 800 years. The mines of **Golden Dagger** and **Vitifer**, (the last productive mines on the moor) were worked until early 20th century. Though little remains of the mining infrastructure except for its building foundations, this fascinating area reveals the scale of the open cast mining operation as veins of ore were excavated deep into the hillsides.

Alternative return routes

The quick route continues straight ahead (N), retracing the steps of Option **(b)**, climbing steadily up the valley through the mine workings directly back to **Bennett's Cross**.

However, if refreshment at **The Warren House Inn** is attractive, we turn left to climb steeply up the valley side. From the top the path, winding its way through the heather to the pub, is clearly visible (Wp.16 141M). From there, we stroll along the roadside to **Bennett's Cross** and the car (Wp.17 152M), with good views of the walled fields on the flanks of **Birch Tor** ahead (known locally as the **Four Aces**); local legend claims that the Devil had a hand in their making.

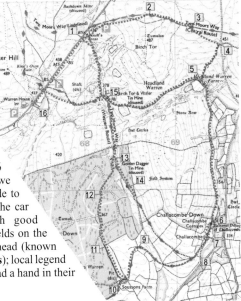

This walk - one for a good clear day - starts with a steady climb past some gorgeous craggy tors as we anticipate fabulous views from the top of **Hamel Down**. We take in some modern and some exceedingly ancient history on our way up, and at the top revel in a sense of freedom and glorious space as we stride out across the open moor. A quick drop down brings us back to **Widecombe** where we recommend exploring the superb church before visiting one of the pubs or cafés for welcome refreshment.

Access by car:
Park in **Widecombe** in the car park directly opposite the church.

Facing the handsome church and leaving the car park (Wp.1 0M), we turn right alongside the village green and right again on the tarmac road towards **Natsworthy** (Wp.2 2M).

A gradual uphill stretch for 2½ miles on the road (usually fairly traffic free) makes for a pleasant warm up prior to the stiffer climb on the moor. As we stroll past fields and woods by the **East Webburn River** we can pick out (on our right) firstly the big, knobbly mound of **Bonehill Rocks** with its square turret on top and then, following on to the north, the tors of **Bell**, **Chinkwell** and **Honeybag**. We come upon **Widecombe Manor** and then **Isaford Farm**, and take in tempting views of **Hamel Down** stretching out on our left - we'll be up there soon. Our road bends left over a stream at **West Lodge** (Wp.3 35M) and a few yards up on the left at a gateway, we can savour the view down to **Widecombe** and get a sense of just how high we've already climbed.

Keeping ahead, we pass **Lower** and **Higher Natsworthy Farms** then, when a high mossy wall with ingrown beech trees runs along our left, we see a clump of trees ahead and a sign leading us on to the moor at **Natsworthy Gate** (Wp.4 52M). Heading towards **Firth Bridge** (NW) and skirting **Heathercombe Plantation** on our right, we see our well-trodden path up onto the open moor. It's quite a steep climb with the views becoming increasingly splendid, especially when looking back. Ahead we can make out the circular **Berry Pound** on the hillside, just to the left of where the **East Webburn River** follows a gully off the moor. After 20 minutes we arrive at an RAF memorial stone, worth further inspection (Wp.5 71M). Take the opportunity to appreciate the massive panorama; **Castle Drogo** to the north and then, following round to the east, **Easdon Tor**, **Hayne Down**, **Hound Tor** with its crags just below the line of the hills, **Haytor** and on across to **Rippon Tor** (SW), with the outcrops of the smaller tors we passed earlier in the foreground. Just splendid!

Leaving the memorial, we head north along a small grassy track which quickly meets up with a broader path where we turn left (Wp.6 75M W). As we head up to the saddle between two rounded hills we can spot **Hookney Tor** ahead with its characteristic square end and the white outline of **The Warren House Inn** in the distance. We begin to drop down, our track broadens and a rough stone wall suddenly appears in front of us. This is a real 'wow' moment - we have arrived at the ancient settlement of **Grimspound** (Wp.7 93M).

It's easy to spend time here either lunching or just mooching, so we've reset our clock timings for the rest of the walk. We set off south (0M), leaving **Grimspound** through its main entrance on quite a steep uphill climb, now on the **Two Moors Way**, our well-used path soon bringing us to the trig point at **Hameldown Tor** where we seem to be on top of the world – we have great views all around and it feels good to be alive! (Wp.8 10M).

Grimspound (a *pound* is a type of enclosure) is thought to have been built about 3500 years ago in the middle Bronze Age. It consists of a substantial wall originally about 9 feet wide and 5 feet high, surrounding 4 acres of land which housed a farming community. The magnificent paved original entrance to the pound would have helped reduce the amount of mud and debris that was brought in, suggesting that animals were taken to the moor for grazing, probably returning at nightfall. Of the 24 huts, at least 13 were inhabited, typically comprising 4 foot high stone walls, a doorway/entrance passage and a central post, or ring of wooden posts, supporting a thatched or turfed roof ; some even had a hearth and cooking pit to complete the home comforts. The remaining huts and structures were probably storehouses or stock pens, and the community was supplied with water by the **Grimslake**, a small stream running through the pound.

It's easy walking as we pass near the remains of **Hamel Down Cross** and then arrive at **Broad Barrow** (the first of three, Wp.9 23M) and, as another track joins us from the left, we continue straight on (S). Now we really appreciate a clear day and clement weather –but the moor can quickly become bleak and unforgiving up here. We follow the ridge over the grassy moorland, taking in **Single Barrow** (Wp.10 28M) and then **Two Barrows** (Wp.11 32M) as a boundary wall comes in on our right. These ancient folk certainly knew how to pick a spectacular burial spot.

Hameldown Beacon

Our route takes us south to **Hameldown Beacon** (Wp.12 37M) and we begin our gentle descent off the moor. When **Widecombe** pops into view we meet a boundary wall coming in from our left, and a signpost at the corner (Wp.13 59M) directs us straight on to 'Widecombe' on this well-trodden track with the wall on our left and the church nestling below.

After 5 minutes our signed path diverges left (Wp.14 64M) and we head downhill (SE), following the wall and stream on a sometimes slippery track to arrive at a gate off the moor (Wp.15 73M). Our way is now a narrow sunken lane which becomes a small tarmac road as it leads us down, often quite steeply, to a T-junction onto the **Natsworthy** road that we walked earlier; we turn right to retrace our steps to **Widecombe** and our car (Wp.16 83M).

Widecombe Church

Widecombe-in-the-Moor is well known for its annual fair, first mentioned in parish records in 1850, which is still held on the second Tuesday in September with 'Uncle Tom Cobley and All'.

But the crowning glory of **Widecombe** has to be its late 14 century church - the 'Cathedral on the Moor' - dedicated to St. Pancras and having a fine tower, 135' high, paid for by the grateful tin miners of the area. Inside, the bosses on the ceiling are beautiful; the three hares sharing just three ears whilst each appearing to have two, is worth searching out. This ancient motif (found in Buddhism, Islam, Christianity and Judaism) is thought to have travelled to Europe from the East along the Silk Road. Widely spread across the country, its meaning is debatable - but undoubtedly it was revered and is perhaps a symbol of fertility.

The famous ancient rood screen should also not be missed and on stepping outside, Church House and Sexton's Cottage are also interesting to visit.

North Bovey is a typical small Devon village, church, pub and village green set in rolling countryside. This is a delightful place to start our walk which climbs steadily along the lanes and across downs into the Dartmoor hinterland visiting the well known stone formations of **Whooping Rock**, **Bowerman's Nose** and **Manaton Rocks** as well as the mysterious **Jay's Grave**. There are splendid views on the way and plenty of places to stop and reflect before returning to the car.

3/4 | 3½ H | 8 miles/13 km | 440m / 440m | 3

Access by car: Leave **Moretonhampstead** on the B3213 towards **Princetown** and take the first left to **North Bovey**. In the village follow signs to the car park just south of the church.

We leave the **North Bovey** car park (Wp.1 0M), turning left on the road then immediately right on a footpath signed 'County Road at Blackaller', skirting the left-hand side of the church-yard.

Shortcut

From **Whooping Rock** (Wp.7) we retrace our steps to the trig point on **Easdon Tor** (Wp.6), then head east through a shallow saddle to a cairn (Wp.25). Continuing east we make our way down the hill through bracken towards the forest. At the corner of a boundary wall (Wp.26) we turn left on a track heading north across the hillside picking up another wall which we follow down to the right to a gate off the moor (Wp.27) Taking the bridle path to **Luckdon** we follow the signed path down the hill eventually passing through a gate onto the road at **Luckdon** (Wp.23) where we rejoin the main walk turning left to **North Bovey** (48 minutes, 2 miles/ 2½km).

We follow the path past the church down onto a road (Wp.2 4M), to head (SW) over a multi-arched bridge across the **River Bovey** and up past cottages on the right. Passing through the settlement of **Yarde** the road forks (Wp.3 11M) and we keep left to **Manaton**, still climbing steadily, with good views of **Bovey Castle** on our right in the valley below. As the road levels out, we take a bridle path left to 'Easdon' (Wp.4 18M) up a stony track between high hedges, views of the moor on our left opening out as we gain height. Soon our track starts to descend and, on the left, we take a narrow path heading up to a metal gate on to **Easdon Down** (Wp.5 32M).

Whooping Rock

Easdon Tor lies directly ahead (SE) as we make our way up over the rough ground, following sheep and pony tracks towards the clearly visible trig point (Wp.6 48M). **Whooping Rock** (Wp.7 53M), which lies south of the trig point, is best visited during a gale when the wind is said to make a whooping noise as it whistles through the cracks.

Jay's Grave

This is the grave of a young farm girl Kitty Jay who, according to local folklore became pregnant after a liaison with the landowner's son and hanged herself when he refused to marry her. To ward off evil spirits the locals buried her at this crossroads where three parishes meet, in an attempt to confuse the Devil who would not know which road to take. An intriguing part of this sad tale is that to this day flowers are regularly placed on the grave by an anonymous soul or spirit!

We descend (SE) to a rocky outcrop (Wp.8 64M) and then on down to a track and left through a gate in the corner of the boundary walls (Wp.9 68M), off the moor. The stony track soon becomes a lane as we pass **Barracot Cottage** on the left before arriving at a T-junction (Wp. 10 74M) where we go right for a pleasant mile-and-a-half stroll along the lanes, passing **Heatree Cross** where we turn left to walk alongside **Cripdon Down** to **Jay's Grave** (Wp.11 102M). Our walk now takes us left through a gate, (E) on a bridleway along the right hand side of a boundary wall, gently rising over a small hill from where we first pick out the impressive column of granite known as **Bowerman's Nose**.

Bowerman's Nose

Passing through three more gates, we follow the path across fields down to the road to **Hayne Down** (Wp.12 113M) where we turn left and immediately negotiate yet another gate on to the moor. We now strike out for **Bowerman's Nose**, jutting up on the skyline, following a marked bridle path heading (NE) up the hill. The rock is even more imposing close to (Wp.13 123M), and it's easy to believe the local legend that Bowerman, a bowman at the time of the Norman conquest, had an encounter with the Devil when out hunting one night.

Leaving the rock pillar we climb steeply (SE) to the tor above (Wp.14 128M) finding at the summit an undulating grassy area surrounded by plenty of rock shelter, an ideal place for a picnic. From here we head (SE) into a shallow saddle, where we locate a well trodden track which we follow left (ENE) down the hill. As we reach the boundary of the moor, we skirt a wall on our left passing a blocked off *sheep creep* to stroll on through a wooden gate (Wp.15 139M) into scrubby woodland where we descend quite steeply. As we pass a house, **Hayne**, we join a lane and after 100 yards take a footpath over a stile to our left (Wp.16 146M), heading across a meadow towards **Manaton** church on the hill opposite.

Making for the thatched roof of **Mill Farm**, we leave the field to its right (Wp.17 149M), turning left on the road crossing **Hayne Brook** and then embarking on the stiff climb up to **Manaton** crossroads (Wp.18 154M). Carrying straight on up a broad avenue of trees towards the church we turn left through a splendid lych gate into the churchyard past grave stones to an exit gate (Wp.19 158M). We follow signs to 'Langstone' along a narrow fenced corridor across private land, appreciating the unusual gorse topiary on our left.

Our path negotiates several ladder stiles and then zigzags steeply uphill through woodland. At the top we divert right, clambering up boulders on to **Manaton Rocks** (Wp.20 168M) from where we get stunning panoramic views, **Lustleigh Cleave** (E), **Haytor** (S), **Hamel Down** (SW), and **Easdon Tor** (NW). We carefully descend, climbing over a stile at the rock base, heading (NW) down through bracken then swinging right into woodland to a T-junction (Wp.21 178M). Our track takes us left over a stile, alongside a boundary wall at the edge of a field, then forks right over yet another stile into an area of ancient woodland - moss clad rotting tree trunks covered in ferns and branches dripping with lichen - and we must tread carefully across stepping stones laid in the swampy ground

We leave the wood over a stile and stream, following a well defined sheep track uphill (N) across a field, exiting right through a gate (Wp. 22 192M) on to a lane. At **Langstone Farm** the lane swings left and we then have a one and a half mile hike past **Luckdon** (Wp.23 200M) and **Aller Mill** and over the picturesque **Fairbrook** double bridge back to **North Bovey**, reaching the car park just before the village green (Wp.24 213M).

The Ten Tors was conceived in 1959 by three Army Officers as a challenge for young people, the Armed Services being well used to the rigours of Dartmoor. Youngsters grouped into teams of six must walk a route over ten specified tors in two days in this wild, arduous terrain. Distances of 35, 45 or 55 miles are covered by different age groups from 14 up to 20 years, the event being co-ordinated and carefully supervised by a collaboration of the Armed Services.

Thankfully, our walk is not quite in this league (25 miles less than even the shortest walk!) but we do pass ten *tors* and it is a rewarding expedition – good climbs, great views, beautiful countryside and fascinating historical interest.

4 | 4H | 9½ miles/15 km | 520m 520m | | 2

Access by car:

From **Bovey Tracey** take the B3387 towards **Haytor Vale** and **Widecombe**. After ¼ mile turn left to **Haytor** at **Five Wyches Cross**. After 5 miles, fork right to **Hound Tor** and **Manaton** and after a further 1.5 miles, turn right at **Swallerton Gate** and park immediately on the left.

> **Shortcut**
>
> For just Seven Tors, follow the route to Wp.20 and keep to the right on the track, picking up the main route again at Wp.24 (3.5 hours, 8 miles/13 km)

It's impossible to miss **Hound Tor** from the car park (Wp.1 0M) and after a pleasant little warm up climb (SE), we arrive at the rocky crags which we pass between, rather like strolling up the nave of a magnificent roofless cathedral (Wp.2 7M). Walking straight on, we make for the just visible outlines of the famous medieval village below, following a clear path through bilberries, bracken and, in springtime, a haze of bluebells.

Hound Tor

Hound Tor Medieval Village

It is known that a fair sized farming community flourished at **Hound Tor** around 1300AD. At least three of the 11 buildings on this typical sloping site were longhouses, providing single storey living quarters for people at the upper end and animals at the lower, a convenient drain being placed in these quarters. The largest longhouse (17.5 x 4 metres) is sited furthest from **Hound Tor**. It is suggested that the hamlet was deserted at the time of the Black Death around 1348, although climate change has been mooted as another possible reason for its decline.

Leaving the settlement (Wp.3 15M) with **Greator** close by on our right (yes, we do count this as one of our ten) we head east and up to a small gate signed to 'Leighon'. We continue straight on, our path narrowing as we drop down into woodland and a second gate; **Haytor Down** looms ahead but first we must cross **Becka Brook** (Wp.4 24M).

Over the water, our well-trodden path winds uphill, and just as we emerge from the woodland (ignoring a small track to the right) we very quickly come to a signpost and boundary stone (Wp.5 30M).

Aiming eventually for **Smallacombe Rocks** above, we set off (ESE) uphill, **Black Hill** to our left, on an indistinct track climbing steeply, soon joining up with a more obvious path leading to the top of the rocks (Wp.6 43M). Here we find a stone circle (in fact, a group of hut circles), fabulous views of the twin peaks of **Haytor** and the main **Smallacombe** crags over to our right. **Holwell Quarries**, our next destination, now appear to the south-west.

We set off on a small grassy path guarded by a fascinating gargoyle-like stone down through a dip to join the track of an old tramway as it cuts across the hillside (Wp.7 51M).

The beehive hut at Wp.8

Following the granite rails right through abundant evidence of quarry workings, we then curve round to the left to find an intact beehive hut, a quarryman's shelter, just below the track on our right (Wp.8 58M).

The tramway continues over a gully and then ends, while we keep going, initially contouring round **Holwell Tor** on narrow paths and then, after about 200 yards, make the ascent, turning left (E) (Wp.9 64M) and clambering upwards. At the top (Wp.10 69M) we pause for breath - with breathtaking views of **Haytor** - and set off, drawn irresistibly to those massive granite rocks. We pick up a broad grassy track crossing one tramway, then coming to a second (Wp.11 73M), follow it as it runs below to the head of a small disused quarry. Our route takes us on a gentle incline to the gap between the two enormous outcrops of **Haytor** (Wp.12 83M). Rock climbers find many a challenge here, and even at our level the views are simply stunning.

Only six tors to go!

We turn right, going round the back of the main *tor*, and step carefully down a steep section making for a clear path leading (SW) to **Saddle Tor**, looking back to enjoy the sight of the sphinx-like silhouette of the rock. From the summit of **Saddle Tor** (Wp.13 100M) we have easy walking down a broad track to the road (Wp.14 105M) and turn right alongside it on a grassy path, thus avoiding any traffic. At a cattle grid (Wp.15 112M) and road junction (**Hemsworthy Gate**) we walk on for a few more yards up the road turning left on the well-used footpath leading (W) up to **Top Tor**.

About two-thirds of the way up (Wp.16 117M), we branch out left (SW) on sheep tracks looking out for remains of the ancient settlement of **Foale's Arrishes** on the slope below (very difficult to see through summer bracken). We bear round west to **Pil Tor** which rises on the skyline and, climbing up to it, find lovely sheltered rest spots and viewing points (Wp.17 126M). Time slips away up here on a fine day.

The next section of our walk takes us broadly north climbing up and down over a number of lovely tors, fortunately all quite close to each other.

We set off for **Top Tor** (NE) which appears to consist of three outcrops; aiming to the left of the right hand one works well and our path is certainly not virginal. From the top (Wp.18 132M) we can easily pick out our next track and clamber down to it, heading a little west of north to **Bonehill Down** and the tors beyond. We have a good stretch out now, crossing the main road to **Widecombe** and then coming down to a lane at the base of **Bonehill Rocks** (Wp.19 147M).

This is a popular spot, certainly because it's a great place for a scramble over a chaos of rocks but also, we suspect, because it's easily accessible by car!

Continuing over the rocks, we turn left at the lane. As it leaves the open moor through stone gateposts we turn right (Wp.20 153M) on a stony track. This is the point to take the shortcut (by keeping on this track, NE) if the prospect of another three tors is a bit daunting. We however bear left, hugging the wall for a few yards, then striking out to the right (N), towards **Bell Tor** rising ahead. It's quite a slog uphill on the grassy track to the summit (Wp.21 161M), then another quick climb brings us to **Chinkwell Tor** (Wp.22 169M) - great views from up here! At last our final tor beckons. We continue north for one more short, steep ascent and, hurrah, we've made it. **Honeybag Tor** welcomes us for a rest and sit down (Wp.23 177M).

Holwell Lawn

Retracing our steps now over **Chinkwell** we make for **Bell Tor** (Wp.21 189M) where we fork left (SE) in the direction of **Haytor** which rises in the distance. Our grassy path takes us downhill, past a pond on our right to a track T-junction (Wp.24 194M) and we turn left soon coming down to a road (Wp.25 198M). Turning left, we cross a cattle grid, climbing over a stile on the right before reaching a small copse, into **Holwell Lawn** (Wp.26 203M), a mass of beautiful bluebells in May.

We walk for a few yards parallel to the trees on our left then bear right (E) on the permitted path across this delightful meadow, then through an area equipped with horse jumps to a gap in the wall ahead (Wp.27 211M). Turning left along the wall and swinging round towards **Hound Tor**, we negotiate a gate and, keeping left, head off just to the left of the tor on a well-worn path. After about 10 minutes and almost in line with **Hound Tor**, we detour briefly to the left (SW) for one last point of interest - an ancient *cist* and stone circle (Wp.28 229M), before returning to our car, and a well-deserved cup of tea from **The Hound of the Basket Meals** at **Swallerton Gate** (Wp.29 238M).

15 AROUND ILSINGTON

This is a great walk for springtime. The wild flowers are absolutely beautiful – primroses, violets, anemones, celandines and bluebells - the hedgerows and woods are brimming with them. And when the weather is not so good higher on the moor, this walk offers a chance for a breath of fresh air in more sheltered hills, woods and valleys on pretty and tranquil tracks and lanes.

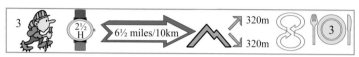

Access by car: From **Bovey Tracey** take the B3387 towards **Haytor Vale** and **Widecombe**. After ¼ mile turn left to **Haytor** at **Five Wyches Cross**. Continue for 3 miles and turn left to **Ilsington**, going over a cattle grid and straight on. A further 1½ miles brings us into **Ilsington**; park by the church.

Stroll

This is the first loop of the figure of eight. Follow the route from the start to Wp.9 (which is the same as Wp.22). Return to the car at Wp.23 (2½ miles/4km, 1 hour 10 mins).

We start from **St Michael's Church** facing the telephone box (Wp.1 0M) and turn immediately right down a lane keeping the church on our right and the Junior School to our left. Coming to a junction at **The Carpenter's Arms** (Wp.2 1M) we walk left out of the village down **Old Town Hill** and just as it becomes steep we leave the road to the left over a stile (Wp.3 6M).

Following the signs we bear right on a permitted path through a charming bluebell wood and take the small leafy path down the hill exiting the trees at a stile to a road (Wp.4 12M). We carry straight on into a small lane, crossing **Liverton Brook** and up the hill the other side. Towards the top we turn right at the crossroads (Wp.5 17M) along **Tipleyhill Lane**, a farm track along a ridge with pretty views and lovely wild flowers.

After 10 minutes, as the track curves left, we take a sharp right turn (Wp.6 27M) downhill on an old, stony and sometimes muddy track, alongside woods and fields. After re-crossing the brook, we come to a road and turn right (Wp.7 34M). Our way is to the left ahead, but take care crossing the road on the bend over to **Lenda Lane** (Wp.8 36M).

We stroll uphill on another charming section, accompanied by gorgeous flowers and handsome views as **Haytor** appears in the distance to the right. At a cross tracks (Wp.9 54M) we head left (S) downhill towards the **Lounston** settlements, then right at the lane soon facing us (Wp.10 57M). Two minutes further on at **Great Lounston Farm** (Wp.11 59M) the lane swings right and we continue straight ahead on a small track past a sign to 'Halford Cross, Rora, Ramshorn Down' and the houses of **Lower Lounston**.

... another charming section ...

The path meanders up and down through the tranquil countryside - the only traffic is rabbits - with yet more flowers and, as it narrows, even orchids can be spotted nestling at the wayside. Over a stile (Wp.12 74M) we keep to the boundary hedge on our right, down a grassy field into managed woodland with a stile and stream at the bottom. Negotiating the stepping stones, we turn left (Wp.13 77M) on a small earthy path with the stream on our left, heading to **Woodgate Cottages**. Our track becomes a garage driveway which bears left at the cottages with two paths to the right (Wp.14 87M) heading into woodland.

The muddy track at Wp.17

We fork right to 'Ramshorn Down', then over a stile and through a small clearing across a forestry road heading up into conifer woodland. A gentle climb quickly brings us to a junction of several tracks (Wp.15 90M). The main track continues round to the right in the trees, but we bear left off the main track on a path leading uphill (SW), skirting the conifers to our right. After 200 yards the track splits again (Wp.16 93M) and we fork left, still keeping out of the conifers. Bearing round to the left, we come almost immediately to a gate and keep straight on (S) down to a junction on a muddy track, well-used by horses (Wp.17 98M).

Ignoring the gate ahead, we turn right on a public footpath, gradually gaining height with open fields and occasional gorse patches on our right. A rounded grassy field opens out in front of us with great views as we continue up towards bracken and trees at the southwest corner of the field. At a signpost

Ramshorn Down

(Wp.18 105M) we take the path to the left, passing through a gate after 20 yards and bearing right at a fork to **Ramshorn Down** (Wp.19 107M). We now have a steady ascent on a broad stony track amidst gorse onto more exposed terrain and the highest point of our walk with good views all round.

As we descend we meet a lane at right angles (Wp.20 117M) and turn right, heading directly for **Haytor** in the distance. We have an easy stroll for two thirds of a mile to a crossroads at a redbrick house (Wp.21 130M) and bear right on a track (which is in fact the other end of **Lenda Lane**). More wild flowers take us to an earlier junction (Wp.22 137M) and a left turn leads us back to **Ilsington**.

A steep section on slippery stone here can be tricky –the earthy track up on the left may be easier – and soon we come to the village where a quick left and a right round the back of the church take us to our car (Wp.23 151M).

Haytor is one of the most famous and well visited tors on Dartmoor; in addition to providing glorious views over South Devon, the area is full of interesting archaeological remains from all eras. We start this walk from the Dartmoor National Park Information Centre and make the short stiff climb to **Haytor Rocks** dominating the skyline. After taking in the views we visit the old granite quarries and the remains of an intriguing tramway then skirt the perimeter of **Haytor Down** before returning via **Haytor Vale** and an opportunity to catch welcome refreshments at **The Rock Inn**.

Access by car: From **Bovey Tracey** take the B3387 towards **Haytor** and **Widecombe**. After ¼ mile turn left to **Haytor** at **Five Wyches Cross**, continuing for 2½ miles and park on the left by the Dartmoor National Park Information Centre.

Haytor Rocks

Across the road from the carpark (Wp.1 0M) we take the well-trodden track steeply up to this distinctive tor, the rocky outcrop resembling a six toed foot emerging from the ground. On reaching the top (Wp.2 11M) we enjoy a well-earned rest while admiring the views across to the south coast.

Continuing (NE), we follow the small grassy path heading for the right hand side of the quarry in the valley.

Haytor Quarry

As we approach we bear left across to the fence running round the top of the quarry (NE) to look down into the old excavation with its heather and gorse covered sides and central pool, then follow the fence right to a gate into the quarry (Wp.3 19M).

Through the gate, we turn left into the sheltered enclosure to explore the old remains of the derrick used to lift blocks onto the tram trucks and securing rings firmly fixed in the rocks, then leaving via a wooden stile over to the right (Wp.4 22M). We head between two spoil mounds (ENE) and join the old granite tramway emerging from the quarry (Wp.5 24M).

Turning left on the tramway we follow the smooth granite as it curves right to join the main tramway at a set of stone points (Wp.6 27M).

Tramway points at Wp.6

We leave the tramway and strike north on a cropped grass track through bracken going gently uphill and cross a path up to an outcrop of rocks on the south-west side of **Black Hill** (Wp.7 39M).

After taking in stunning views west, we head (NE) towards a cairn on top of **Black Hill** (Wp.8 44M), to be confronted with more views north and east over the Devon countryside. From the cairn, our return path can be seen in the distance, contouring round the side of **Haytor Down**.

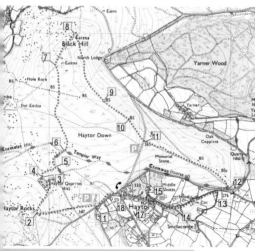

We set off south initially, then take the clearly visible well-worn path dropping down, then swinging left round the hill.

It's easy walking with good views to the left of **Yarner Wood** and **Bovey Tracey** beyond, passing a stone on the left of the path (Wp.9 55M).

Engraved with 'Victoria' one side and 'DS 1853' on the other, it's one of a series of boundary stones erected by the Duke of Somerset (hence the 'DS') around his land in 1853. He chose different names for each, the next being 'Old Jack' (Wp.10 61M).

After **Old Jack** we continue ahead, crossing a lane (Wp.11 64M) and heading down the spur, eventually swinging right and steeply down to the road (Wp.12 76M).

Going right along the road for 20 yards, we turn left at a blue waymark (Wp.13 78M), down to a wooden gate and join a driveway right between the grounds of large houses heading for **Bel Alp House**. The driveway turns to a gravel track, then continues as a bridleway signed 'Haytor Vale' (Wp.14 85M) into woodland through an unusual metal turnstile. We climb through the woods and as the trees end (Wp.15 88M), turn sharply left up steps, through a gate and along a narrow path onto the road (Wp.16 90M).

We're at the back of **The Rock Inn** - straight on up steps and through a passage takes us to a road and the main entrance (Wp.17 92M). From the inn we turn right on the road on a short sharp climb to a T-junction (Wp.18 98M) where we turn right over a cattle grid then, cutting left across the corner verge in front of **Moorlands House**, we return to the carpark (Wp.19 102M).

17 LUSTLEIGH CLEAVE - HUNTER'S TOR

A *cleave* is a steep-sided valley, and at **Lustleigh** the **River Bovey** has carved a spectacular path through colourful, mixed woodland that is ever changing with the seasons. This walk takes us along the length of the cleave, at first tracking the river in the trees, where in springtime the haze of the bluebells in the glades is glorious. We then climb, quite steeply at times, to the upper reaches of the gorge with its massive granite outcrops - and there on the top is an ancient Iron Age hillfort with spectacular views.

Our return takes us to the upper reaches of the river, which we follow downstream, as it drops steeply through a series of cascades, rushing and tumbling through the trees. There are numerous suitable picnic stops available or, for those with different tastes, a very accessible pub!

3	3¼ H	9 miles/14km	350m / 350m		3

Stroll	**Shortcut**
From the car park to **Hisley Bridge** (Wp.3) and across it to Wp.20 and return. (¾ hour, 2 miles/3km)	Follow the route to Wp.7 and turn left down to **Clam Bridge**. Cross the bridge and turn left to join the main route at Wp.18 (1½ hours, 4½ miles/7km)

Segments of this walk can be 'mixed and matched' with those of Walk 18 for real variety around **Lustleigh** at waypoints 1706 and 1718. (N.B. For GPS users, load tracks 17 & 18 and swop over at the above waypoints.)

Access by car:
From **Bovey Tracey** take the B3387 signposted 'Haytor' and follow the road to the right signed 'Manaton'. Take the second turning on the right in the direction of **Lustleigh** and after 1 km, just before crossing over the **River Bovey** at **Drakeford Bridge**, take a left turning along a small dirt track and park the car.

From the carpark (Wp.1 0M) we walk back to the road, turn left over **Drakeford Bridge**, and take the first turning 200 yards on the left signed to 'Rudge and Sanduck'.

... masses of gorgeous bluebells ...

Passing through the gate 100 yards on the left (Wp.2 5M), we enter a field and follow the footpath (SW) alongside the river heading for another gate which takes us into **Bovey Valley Woodland**. We continue in a SW direction walking through very pretty mixed woodland (late spring is the best time to see masses of gorgeous bluebells) along the bank of the fast flowing **River**

Bovey until we reach **Hisley Bridge** (Wp.3 21M). This is a delightful spot – the mediaeval packhorse bridge spans the **Bovey** and used to provide a link for **Lustleigh** to the old **Manaton-Bovey Tracey** road.

Leaving the bridge, we climb steadily NW, parallel to the river but above it, in the direction of **Lustleigh**. The path is quite broad and the woodland rises steeply on the right and soon the track and river start to diverge as we gain height up the side of the valley. The main track takes us to the right (Wp.4 30M), still climbing and after a further 300yds the path splits again and this time we bear left heading for a stile in the boundary wall (Wp.5 36M).

Over the stile, we immediately turn right (N) climbing steeply aided by natural tree root steps until we intersect a path. Our route takes us left to **Manaton**, and in the clearings between the trees we glimpse **Trendlebere Down** across the valley. We ramble on gently in the woodland, ignoring a path forking to the left (Wp.6 44M), then going steeply uphill until we reach a signpost (Wp.7 46M) where we continue up towards **Lustleigh**.

After clambering upwards over boulders for 100 yards alongside a solid granite boundary wall on our right, we continue straight on at a signpost to 'Hammerslake', still on a gentle incline. What looks like a stone circle emerges from the cleared woodland on the left, and we stroll on for a further 200 yards, gradually descending until we reach a T-junction (Wp.8 56M).

Hunter's Tor is our target. We set off left (W) up a steep zigzagging path which winds its way through huge granite boulders with the occasional cave and rock shelter, ignoring a small track to the right that heads off through the boundary.

Mushroom Rock

At the top of **Sharpitor** (Wp.9 65M) we get a spectacular view across the valley with **Hound Tor** silhouetted on the sky line. Still following the boundary wall, we pass an excellent mushroom-like viewing point from which the full extent of the cleave can be appreciated.

Our path continues NW gradually climbing and we finally emerge at the top in open moorland amongst gorse and bracken. We make our way to **Hunter's Tor** (Wp.10 90M) at the northern end of the ridge where we can only just make out the Iron Age fort – but the magnificent 360° panorama more than compensates for this.

Looking south we see the unique outline of **Haytor Rocks** with **Hound Tor** following on clockwise. **Hayne Down** and **Bowerman's Nose** can then be identified, with **Manaton** with its church and rocks further west. Still going round, **Easdon Tor** (W) and **North Bovey** (NW) with the newly redeveloped **Bovey Castle** behind are evident, and then **Moretonhampstead** to the north with moorland behind. To the east we see the beautiful rolling **Devon** countryside which brings us around to the south where on a clear day the coast and **Teignmouth** come into view – and then we are back full circle to **Haytor Rocks** again. What a view!

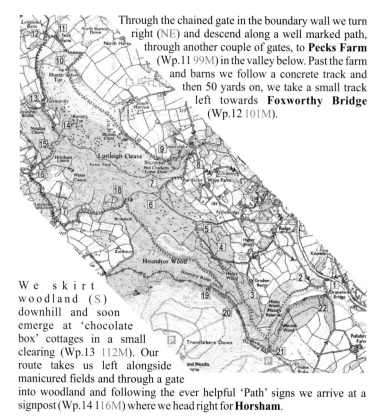

Through the chained gate in the boundary wall we turn right (NE) and descend along a well marked path, through another couple of gates, to **Pecks Farm** (Wp.11 99M) in the valley below. Past the farm and barns we follow a concrete track and then 50 yards on, we take a small track left towards **Foxworthy Bridge** (Wp.12 101M).

We skirt woodland (S) downhill and soon emerge at 'chocolate box' cottages in a small clearing (Wp.13 112M). Our route takes us left alongside manicured fields and through a gate into woodland and following the ever helpful 'Path' signs we arrive at a signpost (Wp.14 116M) where we head right for **Horsham**.

Boulder Bridge

The river draws us near as it rushes and tumbles down and eventually we are confronted by a natural bridge made of massive boulders. Do we really go this way over the river? Yes, we do! The water cascades underneath and bursts out between the granite rocks and we need to take care as we clamber on the slippery mossy surfaces.

Our path takes us left and then upwards as we leave the river, and at our next junction (Wp.15 125M) we continue on to **Horsham** climbing steps up the very steep side of the valley, over a stile and follow a granite wall on our right. We arrive at **Horsham**, keeping left round in front of the first house and, leaving the settlement behind us, continue on our way past a corrugated garage (Wp.16 135M) where we bear left over a ford to **Water**. Striding out now, we come to a crossroads (Wp.17 143M) where we head left, almost veering back on ourselves, for **Lustleigh**. Alternatively, if you're in need of refreshment, then take this quick diversion.

Diversion to Kes Tor Inn
At Wp.17 turn right and follow through the cottages of **Water** for 100 yards. Now take another right for 200 yards down to the main road, and the pub is on your right. When recovered, retrace your steps to the 'cross-tracks' at Wp.17 and continue straight on towards **Lustleigh**.

Clam Bridge

Continuation
After 200 yards we fork left downhill on a sunken stony track and then through a gate we are back into **Bovey Valley Woodland** again. Our path descends over streams and, ignoring a sign to **Becky Falls** on the right, we eventually drop down steeply to **Clam Bridge** (Wp.18 160M).

N.B.GPS reception can be very poor at this point.

We turn right (SE) alongside the river towards **Manaton Old Road** with our well defined and rocky path running closely by the side of the river which descends the valley through a series of very impressive rapids. The wooded sides of the valley are steep - hence poor GPS reception again. After this beautiful stretch our track bends right and heads NW back up the converging **Becka Brook** valley which we cross at a wooden bridge (Wp.19 175M). At the **Manaton Old Road**, heavily used by timber lorries, we turn left towards **Trendlebere Down**, after 250 yards pass **Hisley Bridge** again (Wp.20 180M) (but this time on the other side) and continue on climbing gently.

We divert left off the main track through a gate set back in the trees (Wp.21 188M) into Woodland Trust land, **Pullbrook Wood**, and follow the broad path (NE) down through the wood back to our car (Wp.1 198M).

18 LUSTLEIGH & BECKY FALLS

Lustleigh Cleave is one of the prettiest woodland valleys in the **Dartmoor National Park**. The **River Bovey** and **Becka Brook** meet in the **Cleave** after falling steeply down from the moor The area is crisscrossed by paths providing many walking opportunities but this route is one of our favourites at any time of the year, starting in picturesque **Lustleigh**, crossing the **Cleave** to **Water**, and returning via **Becka Brook**. We still haven't managed to include visits to both of the really good pubs and the tea-shop in a single trip but we're working on it!

Segments of this walk can be 'mixed and matched' with those of Walk 17 for real variety around **Lustleigh** at waypoints 1807, 1809, 1817 and 1819.
(N.B. For GPS users, load tracks 17 & 18 and swop over at the above waypoints.)

Access by car:
Leave **Bovey Tracey** on the A382 towards **Moretonhampstead** and turn left after 3 miles towards **Lustleigh**. Park on the street near the church.

Stroll
Follow the route to Wp.7, turning left down to **Hisley Bridge** Wp.18, then take the route back to **Lustleigh** (70 minutes, 2½ miles/4km)

Shortcut
Follow the route to **Clam Bridge** Wp.9, turning left and following the river down to Wp.17, then following route back to **Lustleigh** (1½ hours, 4 miles/6½km)

We set off (Wp.1 0M) in a clockwise direction round the church, past the **Cleave Inn** and tea-rooms on the left, to a cross roads where we go straight over to a no-through road heading for **Lustleigh** recreation ground. At the end of the lane we turn left through a gate into the park, following the track past a stone throne perched on top of a large boulder engraved with the names of May Queens crowned there in the past.

The May Queen Throne

We leave the field through a gate and continue uphill into a wooded area onto a small road (Wp.2 8M) where we go left then quickly right at a sign post (with white dot) on a narrow track which winds its way uphill between a mixture of private gardens and woodland, emerging onto a steep lane (Wp.3 11M). Turning right, we climb away from **Lustleigh** past pretty thatched cottages, bearing left at **Pethybridge**, then on to another road junction opposite **Cleveland St Mary** where we turn right (Wp.4 16M). Still going uphill, after about 100 yards we find a track on the left sign posted to **Lustleigh Cleave** (Wp.5 18M) which takes us up a small stony path between banks of wild

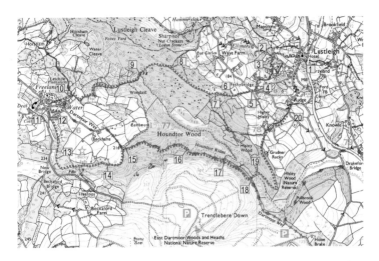

flowers and strawberries (in season), to **Heaven's Gate**, the entrance into **Lustleigh Cleave** woodland (Wp.6 20M).

Our well-defined route heads into the woodland (NW) parallel with a boundary wall on the left, gently descending until at the end of the wall, a track coming steeply uphill joins us from the left, and a signpost indicates that we continue straight on to 'Manaton via Water' (Wp.7 25M). The path meanders through the trees with occasional views across the valley to **Trendlebere Down**, continuing on to 'Manaton via Water' at an intersection (Wp.8 33M). We descend gently through the trees to the **River Bovey** and gingerly traverse the very narrow and slippery tree-trunk crossing known as **Clam Bridge** (Wp.9 38M).

Over the river, we head straight on, steeply up the side of the valley, natural steps helping the ascent in some places, following a mossy stone wall on our right. The gradient gradually eases as the path bears to the right; we ignore a turning on the left to 'Becky Falls' and continue across a stream through a gate up towards **Water**. At a cross-tracks (Wp.10 59M) we go straight on (notice the fine water wheel on the left), and zigzag through cottages, turning right at a road junction up to the main road and the **Kes Tor Inn** - a very suitable stop! (Wp.11 64M).

The water wheel after Wp.10

Refreshed, we're off to **Becky Falls**, heading left (S). One hundred and fifty yards along the main road, we take a path left into a grassy field (Wp.12 66M), following the hedge on the right and leaving the field's right hand corner to enter woodland on a well defined track. Planks take us across the wettest areas, and we catch glimpses of **Becka Brook** on the right. We climb over a

The clapper bridge

stile (look at the lovely little clapper bridge across the brook on the right) and soon arrive at two small gates that take us into the privately owned **Becky Falls Woodland Park** (Wp.13 72M). We continue on the yellow way-marked route, ignoring a turning right, the river gradually gaining speed as it descends into the valley over **Becky Falls**.

Our path wends its way through massive boulders, intersected periodically by the formal walks of **Becky Falls Park**.

We leave the park area (Wp.14 83M), climbing over a stile into **Bovey Valley** and **Hound Tor Woods** onto a wide track high up on the valley side, with the river way down through the trees on the right. At a crossroads (Wp.15 90M) we turn right and steeply downhill on a forestry track, zig-zagging into the valley below, eventually reaching a stone packhorse bridge (Wp.16 103M). Over **Becka Brook** we turn left, still on a forestry track following the brook. Ignoring the next bridge (Wp.17 108M), we stride down to a gate on the left which leads to the sturdy stone **Hisley Bridge** (Wp.18 113M).

Crossing over, we turn left and climb steeply up a short 50 yard slope, then double back right on ourselves (Wp.19 114M) uphill to **Hisley**, winding up the valley side enjoying splendid views of **Trendlebere Down** and **Lustleigh Cleave**. We leave the Woodland Trust on the brow of the hill and start descending on a small track bearing round to the right. We pass through a gate fitted with an interesting improvised shock absorber, and weave our way right and left past a cottage with out-buildings, and turning right down a concrete track, soon arrive at **Rudge** crossroads (Wp.20 134M). We head straight over and down hill to **Lustleigh**, and just before the church, we turn right to find our car (Wp.21 143M) and if you're lucky, either the tea shop or the pub will be open for refreshments.

It's always pleasant to stroll alongside the tranquil waters of a reservoir, and this walk brings us to both **Trenchford** and **Tottiford** - with just a glance at **Kennick**. The sheltered countryside around here is welcoming at any time of year but it's particularly glorious in springtime with beautiful wild flowers at almost every turn. The climb back up from **Christow** through a delightful wooded valley is quite strenuous – but well worth the effort.

Access by car:
From **Bovey Tracey** on the A 382 towards **Moretonhampstead** turn right after 2 miles up a single track road signed 'unsuitable for wide vehicles'. After 0.8 miles turn left at **Pool Mill** crossroads to 'Kennick and Tottiford Reservoir' and 'Moretonhampstead'. Follow the road for 200 yards to a junction and go straight across into **Trenchford Reservoir** carpark.

Short cut
To avoid the climb out of **Christow** (but also missing the pub and pretty woodland), follow the route to Wp.12 and turn right on a public bridle path to **Bowden Farm**, picking up the main route again at Wp.18 (1 hour 50 mins, 5miles/8km).

We start at the information board on the north side of the car park (Wp.1 0M) and follow the pink waymarked route (NW) through trees along the left hand side of **Trenchford Reservoir**. We soon come to the head of the reservoir (Wp.2 7M), with a lovely view down the full length of the lake. Over the bridge, still following the pink way marks, we bear left heading back into woodland. At a T-junction we turn right (Wp.3 10M) up an incline strewn with pine needles. After turning turn sharp right (Wp.4 14M), we quickly come to a stile onto a road (Wp.5 16M).

Crossing the road, we negotiate another stile onto a path (E) signed 'Tottiford Reservoir' and pine woodland gives way to beech on the left as we descend. We turn left at the water (Wp.6 23M) and follow the shore (N) to a bridge with views south down **Tottiford Reservoir** and north to **Kennick Reservoir** dam. Across the bridge, we bear left and after a short climb emerge onto the road (Wp.7 27M).

Tottiford Reservoir

Leaving the reservoirs, we turn right for 150 yards and then head off left (NE) along a footpath heading back into woodland (Wp.8 30M). After 450 yards our path joins a broad stony track (Wp.9 36M) which we follow to the left towards **Clampitt**, dropping gradually to the burial ground (Wp.10 40M).

We set off right on the bridle path passing **Beacon Farm** on our left and at the **County Road** junction (Wp.11 48M) continue straight on to **Christow**.

(After 3 minutes, (Wp.12 51M) our shortcut route takes a right turn on the public bridlepath to **Bowden Farm**).

A gentle climb brings us to the crest of the hill and we enjoy panoramic views ahead to **Haldon Hills** with its white rectangular folly, **Lawrence Castle**.

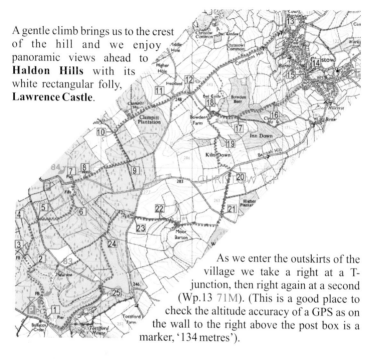

As we enter the outskirts of the village we take a right at a T-junction, then right again at a second (Wp.13 71M). (This is a good place to check the altitude accuracy of a GPS as on the wall to the right above the post box is a marker, '134 metres').

The Artichoke Inn

We stroll into **Christow**, and as **Dry Lane** meets **Wet Lane** (Wp.14 77M), turn right.

Christow offers several refreshment opportunities; **The Artichoke Inn** further down **Wet Lane** could be a good spot for lunch - perhaps worth a quick look?

After 25 yards we come to **Peveril Clematis Nursery** (Wp.15 81M) and struggle to find the Dartmoor National Park Authority sign post on the right which supports a vigorous example of the nursery's trade. The footpath edges round the end of the nursery's boundary wall and follows a small stream uphill past a bamboo screen and then into mixed woodland.

We continue our ascent with the babbling stream on our right following occasional yellow way marks, climbing several stiles.

At a junction (Wp.16 92M) we turn right, picking our way across the stream, then over a ladder stile into a field where we turn left following the edge uphill with the stream now on our left. Another stile takes us back into pretty woodland and we continue uphill, eventually emerging onto a track (Wp.17 103M).

We turn right signed 'Bowden (for Reservoirs)', still climbing and soon see **Bowden Farm** ahead. The track skirts to the right of the farm passing three old millstones, then comes to a sharp right hand bend (Wp.18 108M). Here we go straight ahead through a metal farm gate into a grassy field, bear left still skirting the farm and follow the field edge to a gate into shrubby woodland (Wp.19 114M). Through the gate, we turn right, following the fence then heading left at the corner past a circular cattle trough. From here the path is not very distinct, but the occasional yellow dot is helpful, and eventually we emerge from the scrub into an open field. The path continues along with the fence, then veers left uphill to a stile where we exit the field to a lane (Wp.20 121M).

Crossing over, we head down a grassy byway then, across another road (Wp.21 127M), continue along a track leading to **Moor Barton**. As we approach this delightful farm nestling in the valley, we enjoy lovely views of **Haytor** in the distance. There's no getting lost as we leave heading (W) uphill, as all gates except ours are marked with 'No Entry' signs. As we reach the top the path appears to end, but don't worry; a small metal gate to the right leads us on our way (Wp.22 137M). Our track can be rather overgrown, but we soon step out on to a road and turn right then quickly left over a stile, keeping left as indicated to **Tottiford Reservoir**.(Wp.23 142M).

The grassy byway

The grassy path leads us (SW) through gorse and immature pine, heading off downhill towards the reservoirs. Ignoring a path to the right, we progress down the hill and on reaching the water, carry on across the causeway (Wp.24 149M). Turning left, we follow the water's edge flanked by rhododendrons. On coming to the road (Wp.25 158M), we turn left between the two reservoirs and our road swings right signed 'Reservoirs' with parking in half a mile. Strolling along this peaceful lane, we cross another dam and turn immediately right on a small track which brings us back to the car park (Wp.26 169M).

To quote the Wildlife Trust at the entry point to this walk - "A beautiful river, shady woodland, colourful flowers and loads of wildlife - **Dunsford** really has got the lot". For 'Dunsford' read the **Teign** valley and experience a perfect one-way walk for all seasons. The wild daffodils on the first stretch are glorious in springtime, the dappled glades and dreamy riverside are delightful in summer and the possibility of spotting salmon leaping is enticing in autumn. And for a sheltered winter's expedition with a bus ride for fun - this is the one!

Note: GPS reception is poor along the gorge.

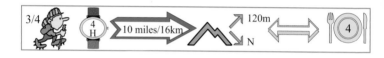

Access by bus:
Take the N°173 from **Chagford** square to **Court Street** car park in **Moretonhampstead** to connect with the N°359 to **Steps Bridge** (complete journey time approximately 35 minutes).

The bus drops us in the car park opposite the **Youth Hostel** (Wp.1 0M) from where we set off, turning left on the road for 300 yards, watching for traffic, past the tea-room (open July and August) and over **Steps Bridge**.

The River Teign, and daffodils

Immediately on the left is our path through a gap in the wall (Wp.2 3M) into trees and we make our first acquaintance with the beautiful **River Teign** on our left.

Mixed woodland, sunny glades of glorious spring flowers and the gliding river make for an entrancing stroll - and there are some great spots to relax too. We prefer to walk down by the water (rather than on the bridle-path to the right) eventually exiting a clearing into woodland where we curve away from the river to a wooden gate and a road (Wp.3 37M).

Turning left along the quiet country lane, we climb gently to **Clifford Cross** (Wp.4 45M) and turn left again down to the river and across **Clifford Bridge**. The lane takes around to the right and opposite smart houses we find a stile and metal gate on the right leading into what's described as 'Fingle - Private Woodland' (Wp.5 49M), however, the path is public and so we make our way into the coniferous woodland.

After 13 minutes the dramatic sounds of **Upperton** weir draw us along a narrow fork for 2 minutes off to the right, to find a pleasant little resting spot with the luxury of a seat, from where we can contemplate the tranquil river upstream, the sea trout pool and water crashing over the weir (Wp.6 65M).

Returning to the main track, we continue alongside the river, ignoring the blue path heading off to the left up to **Wooston Castle** fort (Wp.7 81M). It was just around here we came across spawning frogs in February - spectacular!

Frogs!

Tumbling water and birds make good company as we amble on, with the chance of seeing a kingfisher while dippers and acrobatic wagtails entertain us. It's easy walking on the well-used path alongside the almost textbook-pretty **Dartmoor** river, the gorge becoming ever steeper as we go.

Fingle Bridge

Leaving the private 'Fingle' woodland through a gate we come across the ruined remains of **Fingle Mill**, once used to grind corn with its *leat* running out to the river, eventually arriving at a grassy area and **Fingle Bridge** (Wp.8 111M), a great spot for picnic, paddling or pub - and even rounders if you're that way inclined.

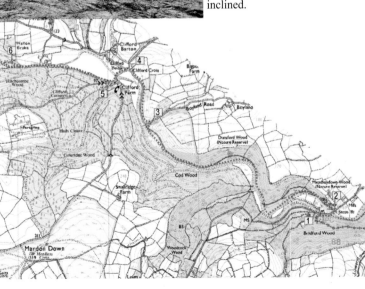

A diversion up the signed footpath to 'Cranbrook Castle fort'(S) is an option at this point for those in need of a challenge, while our way is across the ancient packhorse bridge, enjoying the view of **Prestonbury Castle** fort which dominates the **Fingle Bridge Inn** opposite; refreshments at the inn are always tempting.

After the inn, or if you've resisted it, we turn left along the yellow waymarked **Fisherman's Path** into the National Trust **Castle Drogo Estate**, meandering with the river to **Fingle Weir** - a lovely spot. We stroll on in the deeply wooded gorge through patches of rhododendrons, the path taking us high at times, the river rushing below over moss clad boulders.

A short, steep climb takes us onto the blue limestone of **Sharp Tor** towering above, helpful metal handrails easing our descent and leading us on past scree slopes towards calmer water. We pass the little **Castle Drogo** turbine house to come to salmon pools at **Drewe's Weir** - and here, in late October/November after heavy rain, the sight of salmon and sea trout leaping up the pans is just amazing.

Continuing our stroll, after one minute we come to a suspension bridge and track junction (Wp.9 150M) and go ahead on the **Two Moors Way** through a gate into meadows, losing both trees and gorge. **Castle Drogo** sits behind us, above and to the right, but we follow the river onwards to **Dogmarsh Bridge** and the A382 (Wp.10 161M).

Taking care crossing the road, we follow the path straight ahead, the river still on our left, to a small wooden footbridge into woodland, following signs to 'Rushford Mill' and 'Chagford'.

On a small island just past a weir we discover an intriguing sculpture by Peter Randall-Page; reminiscent of a split walnut, it's called 'Granite Song', is 70cm high and was created in 1991 (Wp.11 169M, see the picture on the following page).

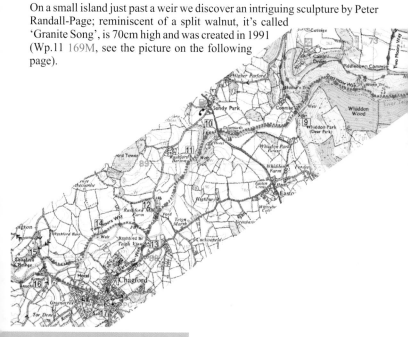

We leave the woods coming to meadowland, with lovely views of **Chagford** church nestling below **Meldon Hill** in front and head towards the barns of **Rushford Mill Farm**, entering the farmyard over a stile. Lethal-looking stepping stones to the left (not to be advised, especially after heavy rain) offer one return route but we make for the road by the farmhouse (Wp.12 180M).

We turn left past the open-air swimming pool to a footpath just before **Rushford Bridge** where we turn right, off the road (Wp.13 184M), signed '2MW'.

Bearing right (N) across the field towards a signpost and gap in the hedge, we turn left to follow the hedge towards trees. We cross a *leat* on a footbridge, continuing with the water on our left until we rejoin the **Teign** at a small weir (Wp.14 193M). The river leads us to meadows through gates and over footbridges on a well trodden route to the road ahead at **Chagford Bridge**, also known locally as **Factory Bridge** (Wp.15 204M).

Turning left on the lane and left again at **Factory Cross** (Wp.16 206M), we have a steep little return climb through the outskirts of **Chagford** back to **Chagford Square** (Wp.17 236M).

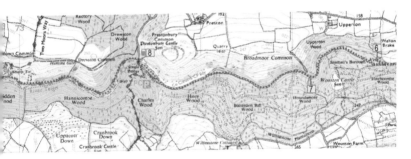

Of all the walks from **Fingle Bridge**, we particularly enjoy this one as it allows us to experience all aspects of this picturesque gorge. It takes in hills, river, woods and heathland, an ancient bridge and a modern castle with magnificent views thrown in along the way. What more could you want!

2	2¼ H	5½ miles/9km	200m / 200m		3

Stroll	**Short version**
Across **Fingle Bridge** following **Fisherman's Path** along the river to Wp.5 via Wp.11 and back. (1 hour, 3 miles/5km)	Don't cross the bridge at Wp.5, but continue left along the riverbank on **Fisherman's Path** towards Wp.11 (1½ hours, 4miles/6½km)

Access by car:
Fingle Bridge is clearly signed from the square in **Drewsteignton** (1 mile). Park alongside the lane near the **Fingle Bridge Inn** pub car park.

We start on the ancient **Fingle Bridge** (Wp.1 0M), as apart from getting our bearings and admiring the river, the **Fingle Bridge Inn** can be eyed up for refreshments later. Leaving the bridge behind us with the pub on our right, we walk back past the cars and turn left after 150 yards along **Hunters' Path** (Wp.2 3M).

Castle Drogo was the last castle built in England. Conceived by wealthy businessman Julius Drewe, whose ancestry claimed a relationship with the Norman baron, Drogo de Teign, he dreamt of a castle as his ancestral home and so commissioned architect Sir Edwin Lutyens to design a spectacular building for him. Commenced in April 1911, it was completed in 1931. Given to the National Trust by the Drewe family in 1974, the house, gardens and tea rooms are open to the public. Well worth a visit.

The stony track takes us uphill on quite a steep incline (GPS reception poor) through mixed woodland predominantly of spindly oak, to the top of the 100 yard climb (15M), where views open out along the **Teign Gorge** towards **Dartmoor**, and we catch our first glimpse of **Castle Drogo**, set on the headland. The path meanders along the top of the gorge through a mixture of clearings and wooded areas, providing glimpses of the steep drop into the gorge below and sounds of the babbling river, our route well marked with signposts indicating 'Hunters' Path'. The gorge face becomes sheer, **Sharp Tor**'s rocky outcrops offering spectacular viewing points; the best is reached after a small stretch of woodland and a gentle incline, leading to an excellent limestone outcrop (Wp.3 30M) where we can take a well earned break enjoying magnificent views of the gorge, castle and **Dartmoor** beyond.

Continuing on **Hunters' Path**, we pass a right hand turning to **Castle Drogo** and its gardens, while our route continues straight ahead, gently swinging right then left amidst heather and gorse in front of the castle squatting on the top of the hill. Views soon open up to the west and south; we see **Chagford** (SW) nestling in a patchwork of fields below **Meldon Hill**, with clear views of the opposite side of the gorge which we'll encounter later. At the end of the gorge the path swings right down another valley below the **Castle Drogo** battlements. The descent moderates through a thickly wooded section to a swing gate where we meet a small single track tarmac lane (Wp.4 45M) where we turn left alongside a small brook on our right, crossing over a cattle grid before leaving the lane, forking left on a track signed the 'Two Moors Way'. The path descends gradually by three handsome Scots pine trees, and alongside the garden of the small thatched cottage of **Gibhouse**.

The River Teign

After a further 200 yards we reach the **River Teign** where it is spanned by a splendid modern suspension bridge, the centre of which (Wp.5 55M) affords us views of a classic Dartmoor river. Crossing the river and clambering over the step built into the large mossy granite wall opposite, we turn right on the grassy track on the other side.

Whiddon Deer Park
Site of Special Scientific Interest
and
Conservation Area of National Importance
The **Whiddon Deer Park** comes under the auspices of the **National Trust** and is an area of special scientific interest and national importance. Its ancient wood pastures are home to a number of nationally rare invertebrates, lichens and plants, and provide sanctuary to a herd of Fallow Deer. There are no public rights of way, but the **National Trust** are happy to allow a low level of access. We ask you to respect the special nature of the park, and to visit only as individuals or couples. Please stay on the route, and be extra vigilant to avoid disturbing the wildlife.

Now in **Whiddon Deer Park**, we follow the main track parallel to the wall (S) as the path opens and curves right and then straight ahead, avoiding the right hand fork in the path which passes over a low arched bridge and gate beyond. We reach a junction as the track is framed by two sycamore trees (Wp.6 65M), and take the smaller grassy path to the left up an incline, underneath overhead electricity supply. The path becomes overgrown, quite narrow and winding, until we reach an enormous fallen tree stump where another track joins us from the right – we go straight on until we reach the boundary wall that converges with our path from the right (Wp.7 70M).

Ignoring a small track straight ahead, we bear left and climb the zigzagging path up through the woodland, emerging at the top to a clearing with a square stone shelter (Wp.8 80M), a tranquil resting spot alongside to enjoy a superb

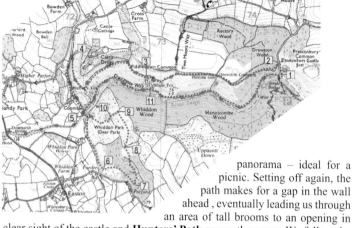

panorama – ideal for a picnic. Setting off again, the path makes for a gap in the wall ahead , eventually leading us through an area of tall brooms to an opening in clear sight of the castle and **Hunters' Path** across the gorge. We follow the path in the direction of the castle to a wall (Wp.9 85M) over which we view the gorge from a different aspect before turning left, following the boundary in a westerly direction heading towards a break in the wall between some large beech trees (Wp.10 87M).

A fascinating sculpture (Passage 1992),fashioned in granite and lead by local craftsman Peter Randall-Page, sits at the base of the first trees of a glorious avenue through which we proceed. The path gets quite steep, turning into a small dirt track with loose stones – a walking stick might come in handy here.

Passage 1992

At a large old ash tree where the track divides (165 yards on from Wp.10) we go right. Ignoring a small turning to the left (200 yards from Wp.10) we keep bearing right until we clamber down, reaching a wall and returning to the suspension bridge crossed at Wp.5. We now retrace our steps across the bridge and join the **Fisherman's Path** on the north side of the river, turning right this time towards **Fingle Bridge**, the river alternately gliding and gushing alongside us. We pass **Drewe's Weir** with its salmon pools, and then the little **Castle Drogo** turbine house. Just when you think the going's easy, we find a flight of stone steps up a small cliff (Wp.11 110M), seemingly designed for people with very long legs – you need to be surefooted here. Our track continues along the river through stretches of wild rhododendrons, with occasional climbs avoiding the rocks below. At a division in the path we can take either route which eventually converge again at **Fingle Weir** at a bend in the river. A good spot for daydreaming, occasionally disturbed by the sound of fish jumping for flies – or perhaps they're doing it just for fun? We are now five minutes easy stroll away from the kissing gate at **Fingle Bridge** where we rejoin our car (Wp.12 135M).

22 MARDON DOWN & BLACKINGSTONE ROCK

We fancied some 'high-up' walking with good views one day – but the weather was a bit unpredictable and we didn't want to be too exposed. This little trek from **Moretonhampstead** just seemed to fit the bill. Our walk begins with a steady climb onto **Mardon Down** with its broad open views, then heads round east and over to the woods at **Westcott**. On our return we come across the two famous massive lumps of granite of **Heltor** and **Blackingstone Rocks** and take in even more stupendous views. (This route has two short sections on busy roads; take care at these points.)

Access by car:
Park in the clearly signed public car park in **Moretonhampstead** just down from the main crossroads in the centre of town on the **Princetown** road (B3212).

Moreton Almshouses

We turn left from the car park in **Moretonhampstead** (Wp.1 0M) towards the centre of town. At the junction by the **Bell Inn** we take **Cross Street** to the right to stroll on past almshouses. At a gate on the left we enter a field (Wp.2 5M) and keeping to the right with the church behind us, head through the gate opposite.

The trail swings round left and steeply down to a stile (Wp.3 12M) where a sign to 'Yarningale' takes us alongside a house and garden on the left to a narrow kissing gate. Passing a garage and greenhouse, we emerge at a T-junction (Wp.4 14M).

Our path to the right quickly shrinks to a narrow earthy track uphill, with a stream below to our right. Negotiating a stile into a small copse brings us almost immediately to a gate and crossroads (Wp.5 18M); still following white waymarked signs for 'Yarningale' we go up the muddy track ahead, keeping to the left of the pigsties. Over a waymarked stile, our scrubby path becomes enclosed by trees, and soon a metal kissing gate brings us onto a broader track which we join to the left to **Mardon Down**. At **Yarningale Bed & Breakfast** our route takes us right on a peaceful lane (Wp.6 29M); after 100 yards we go left through a wooden gate signed 'bridle path to moor' (Wp.7 32M).

Now the views begin to open up, and soon we're out on the moor (Wp.8 38M) - but still going relentlessly uphill. Crossing a small lane (Wp.9 40M), we head north towards a stone circle (Wp.10 45M). To the east we catch our first glimpse of **Heltor Rock** - an enormous lump of granite with a great fissure in it. Keeping straight on, we pass the stones known as **Giant's Grave** as the track broadens, continuing north-east on a well-worn track down to **Headless Cross** (Wp.11 63M). Our path runs east across the junction, following blue waymarks uphill until we fork left at the top of the plateau (Wp.12 70M).

Now we really stretch our legs as we descend, leaving the moor through a gate onto a narrow track (Wp.13 75M). After six minutes we come to a small settlement, turning right on the concrete road (Wp.14 81M) leading steeply downhill. After 100 yards we divert left on a tiny path (Wp.15 84M), slithering and winding through trees.

Our path is signed through a couple of gates, and soon we negotiate stepping stones over a stream and head to the road (Wp.16 95M). Turning right, we have a 500 yards stretch on tarmac before coming to **Rock Valley Farm**, taking the path directly opposite into **Westcott Wood** (Wp.17 101M). Our yellow waymarked route heads up through the trees and across rock-strewn fields until we drop down to the road in the hamlet of **Westcott**.

We turn left and then fork right (Wp.18 114M), zigzagging sharply uphill - quite a mean

Heltor Rock

little climb - and then stride out on the road until we reach the crest of the hill from where **Heltor Rock** is clearly visible to the left with its partner, **Blackingstone Rock**, over to the right.

The story goes (although as with most Dartmoor legends, there's more than one version) that once the Devil and King Arthur took up position, one at each vantage point, and hurled great rocks at each other. At last they could go on no longer – the impressive **Blackingstone Rock** is said to be King Arthur's final missile whilst the Devil could manage to heave no more than the still substantial **Heltor**.

We continue to **Plaston Green** crossroads (Wp.19 129M), beginning our homeward trek on the small lane to the right. **Blackingstone Rock** plays hide and seek with us through the hedgerows, though we are soon confronted by its massive sheer rock face to our left.

The best approach is to climb a little further along the road and take the left turn (Wp.20 154M) (to a destination at the time of writing unusually called 'OW', probably **Christow**), turning left just 100 yards up the lane onto a grassy track. The views from the top are stunning (Wp.21

Blackingstone Rock, and those steps

158M) but the steps up there are seriously vertiginous – certainly not for the faint-hearted, and peculiarly suited to those with tiny feet.

We return to the junction at Wp.20 and continue on our way, heading west towards **Moretonhampstead** and taking a left turn at **Didworthy** (Wp.22 175M), following the lane round to the right alongside **Pepperdon Down**. At a T-junction we turn right again (Wp.23 185M), converging with another lane after 200 yards (Wp.24 188M) where we turn left, sharply back on ourselves, between stone gate posts.

After 100 yards we climb a ladderstile on the right onto the footpath to **Budleigh Farm** (Wp.25 190M), yellow waymarks confirming our route. We cross the fields, go through a couple of gates and then swing to the right to a stile into old woodland (Wp.26 200M). Our path, indistinct at times but well waymarked, meanders down, exiting the wood to skirt it on the left along a rough grassy track. We keep on down, eventually strolling through the holiday complex of **Budleigh Farm** to the main road (Wp.27 219M).

Taking care, we turn right (this is not a particularly pleasant 300 yards section when there is traffic), turning right towards 'Exeter' and 'Dunsford' just past the remains of **King's Bridge** (Wp.28 222M). We soon reach a junction and bear left to **Moretonhampstead**, finding ourselves once again by the almshouses. With a left turn at **The White Hart**, we are back at our car (Wp.29 234M).

The Two Hills Race is run annually from **Chagford** at Whitsun – a lap of the cricket pitch, straight up **Meldon Hill**, down and up to **Nattadon Common** and then back to the start. About fifty folk compete for this local honour and apparently, 26 minutes is a very good time. We take rather longer than this – and our best excuse is that we take in a few extra sights along the way finding the two ancient crosses at **Week Down**, admiring the panoramic views from **Nattadon** and **Meldon** and finishing with a stroll along **Chagford High Street** where a visit to Webbers and Bowdens ironmongers cannot be missed. It's almost impossible to come out empty handed.

Access by car

Park in **Chagford** car park, just past the church on the right.

Shortcut
Follow the route to Wp.15 and turn right back into **Chagford**. (82 minutes, 3 miles/5km)

We start out from the car park (Wp.1 0M), turning left and then immediately right on the road towards **Yellam**, leaving the outskirts of **Chagford** behind us. In about twelve minutes we pick up our track to the right signed to 'Nattadon' and just a few yards along we clamber over a stile to the left (Wp.2 12M), following the broad track uphill and swinging round with the hedge which we follow to a low stile on the left (Wp.3 16M).

Now there's more of a countryside feel as our narrow path takes us along the side of the valley, across a small brook and immediately up rough steps in a retaining wall into pretty woodland. We climb towards and over yet another stile (Wp.4 23M) and then cross the bridle path on to a grassy track alongside a tall wire link fence. We stroll down to **Yellam** where, at a handsome thatched cottage (Wp.5 28M), we take the road to the right. As we ascend the gentle incline we spot our turning to the right on the crest of the hill, through an old lichen-encrusted gate (Wp.6 31M) into the woods towards **Week Common**.

Our path meanders as we climb through the trees to emerge at the top at a field (Wp.7 36M) where we continue climbing, finding a stile in the hedge on our right (Wp.8 39M). Crossing the stile into **Week Down** common land, we continue quite steeply uphill, following the hedge line left until we meet the road (Wp.9 42M) – and now for a quick diversion to an ancient waymark.

Making our way over the cattle grid to the left, we stroll downhill for just 100 yards to where the reputedly Saxon **Shorter Cross** (Wp.10 44M) nestles in the undergrowth on the left –a beautifully simple stone with its cross in relief on the granite.

Week Down Cross

We retrace our steps to the top of the hill, take in those lovely views again and continue along the road until **Week Down Cross** appears, leaning splendidly, on our right (Wp.11 47M). It's worth having a closer look at the stone before we continue along the road and, ignoring a left turn to **Weddicott**, head towards **Nattadon**.

We soon see a cattle grid ahead and turn left (W) just before it (Wp.12 54M), almost back on ourselves on a broad, well-trodden track up to the top of **Nattadon Common** (Wp.13 57M) where the views are tremendous - although the Dartmoor ponies don't seem very impressed! There seem to be a multitude of possible descents from the summit but we forge off through the gorse and bracken on a small track, down in a westerly direction towards a rocky outcrop (Wp.14 65M), on a line with **Meldon Hall** directly below and the flattened nipple of **Kestor** in the distance.

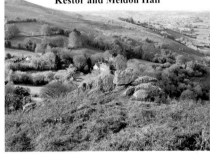

Kestor and Meldon Hall

We zigzag down, quite steeply at times, still towards **Meldon Hall**, then move into trees on an indistinct path to a brook which we negotiate carefully –a stick comes in handy, as we clamber alongside it over rocks and finally emerge onto the road (Wp.15 74M).

Meldon Hill awaits us, and if you don't fancy another climb, now's the time to take a shortcut right on the road back to **Chagford** and the car park. For those determined to conquer both summits, the road takes us around to the left and then we turn right towards **Meldon Common** (Wp.16 77M) and follow the route uphill, ignoring turns to the left and creeping up on **Meldon Hill** from the rear. It's a bit of a slog, but soon the road flattens out as a house appears on the left and we swing round to the right and, where a track crosses the road, we take the broad grassy path up the hill to the right (Wp.17 93M). The trig point soon becomes visible, and we have a superb 360° panorama (Wp.18 101M).

For our route back to **Chagford** we head off (N) for 3 minutes to a nearby rocky outcrop (Wp.19 104M) and see the town laid out clearly below. Just to the right of the rocks we pick up a narrow track for our steep descent (NNE) through the prolific bracken and eventually drop down to **Padley Common** at the bottom of the hill (Wp.20 119M). Carrying straight on, we follow the well-defined track across the grass towards the far corner where, through a gate, we pick up a footpath (Wp.21 121M).

The path skirts round the side of **Chagford** playing fields on our left with marshy scrub to our right and eventually joins a concrete track where we turn right down to the public road (Wp.22 127M). At the road we turn right and climb steadily up to **Chagford High Street** where, in addition to the usual shops, pubs and cafés, we find the 'Aladdin's Cave' stores of Webbers and Bowdens, renowned for stocking everything you could ever want – well worth a visit! We continue along the **High Street** past the square with its octagonal **Market House** and then the parish church of **St. Michael** before arriving back at the car park (Wp.23 137M).

Dartmoor in a nutshell – admittedly a fairly large nutshell as it's quite a step – but this walk has got the lot! We conquer a couple of tors and get tremendous views of that glorious Dartmoor and Devon countryside. We steep ourselves in history with sites that evoke ancient times and former grandeur; a monolith, a pound, stone rows and circles; fascinating. But more than this! We come across rivers and brooks with beautiful clapper bridges, interesting river stones and gorgeous picnic spots. We stroll through woods and forests, country lanes and byways – and there's a great pub only a few yards off the track. A walk not to be missed.

Access by car:
From **Chagford** head south-west along **Manor Road** (a continuation of **High Street** going away from the church), turning right at **Waye Barton Cross** towards **Kestor** and **Thornworthy**. At **Yeo Cross** take the right turn towards 'Teigncombe, Batworthy and Kes Tor' and park after 1.5 miles at **Batworthy**.

From the car (Wp.1 0M) we walk south up the well-used track straight onto the moor with the trees of **Batworthy** on our right. After 200 yards the characteristic flattened nipple of **Kestor** appears to our left and we strike out towards it, turning east (Wp.2 3M) on cropped grass reaching the summit after a brief climb – breathe in that sweet air and take in the great scenery (Wp.3 11M).

Ancient settlement outlines can be made out to the north with splendid distant views of Dartmoor all around. The **Long Stone** is our next target and a small grassy track leads us south-west towards it standing proud on the moor - a substantial

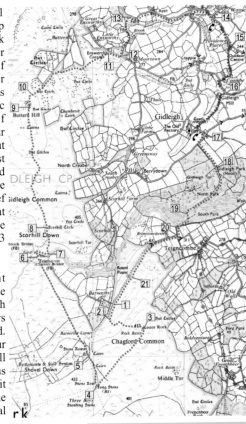

Shovel Down

On the OS map, **Shovel Down** appears as settlements and a field system, together with stone rows and cairns –a bit of an understatement really. The literature offers a variety of interpretations of the ceremonial complex but it undoubtedly has ritual significance. There are at least six stone rows, four of which are double - one of these leads to the 'fourfold circle' consisting of a cairn with four stone retaining rings.

Long Stone

And last but not least, the imposing **Long Stone** forms the endpoint of the south double row and also serves as a boundstone being engraved DC (Duchy of Cornwall), C (Chagford) and GP (Gidleigh Parish). Further south stands a single stone, the only remaining one of the **Three Boys**, said to have been a *dolmen.*

menhir and just a hint of the spectacular remains to come (Wp.4 22M). We set off north, the beginnings of a stone row becoming apparent to our left and, as we drop down we see more rows clearly ahead and veering off to the right – all part of the famous **Shovel Down** complex (Wp.5 28M).

Now we really stretch our legs and step out across the moor aiming for the far corner of **Batworthy** with trees on our right.

North Teign clapper

It's a grassy track on a gentle downhill which brings us to a set of three clapper bridges spanning the **North Teign River** and **Wallabrook** as they rush to converge. Our first is a handsome reconstruction (1999, after the original was swept away by a great flood in 1826) built from two vast granite slabs resting on pier stones over the **North Teign** (Wp.6 46M).

Across and turning right, we follow the flow to explore the second bridge, more modest with metal strapping; the **Teign-e-ver**. Resisting the temptation to cross, we turn round and walk back, following **Wallabrook** running down on our right. This whole area is just delightful – a great place to play, picnic and daydream. Collecting ourselves we continue along the right bank soon coming to the third single slab bridge which takes us across the brook.

Before leaving this site, we have one more famous point of interest to visit

The Teign Tolmen

with a brief detour to the right to locate the **Teign Tolmen**, a fascinating rock with a natural hole right through it. It's said that a climb through to the ledge below is a cure for rheumatism … whooping cough … worth a try? (Wp.7 56M). Clambering up stones with our back to the conifers we continue heading north and soon join the path to **Scorhill Circle**.

Scorhill Circle

This late Neolithic/early Bronze Age monument (Wp.8 64M) is particularly special as it has never been restored. It's superbly located, and there's a great sense of space here. It has a diameter of about 88ft and originally had approximately 65 stones of which 25 now remain standing; a fine example of a stone circle.

Away to the north we can see the low, flattish mound of **Buttern Hill** and aiming for its highest point, we make steady progress across **Gidleigh Common** on tumpy grass. It's quite featureless up here though we pick up sheep and horse tracks now and then, gradually gaining height until we catch sight of the crest of the hill with its few small granite outcrops, our destination (Wp.9 74M). Again we are treated to spectacular views; **Chagford** to the east with its twin hills, **Meldon** and **Nattadon**, **Haytor** in the distance to the south-east, the dark trees of **Fernworthy Forest** to the south, while a great array of somewhat bleak looking Dartmoor hills and tors take us round to the north.

From the summit we bear right (NNE) for 100 yards (Wp.10 76M) and then right again (NE) downhill through the remains of more hut circles towards a boundary wall. Keeping the wall over on our left, we drop down diagonally towards gorse and water, avoiding boggy patches, picking the best route on the day, and soon coming to a T-junction by **Ensworthy Cottage** (Wp.11 95M).

Our route takes us to the right on a tarmac lane for 2 minutes and then we turn left, clearly signposted to 'Aish', (Wp.12 96M) along the **Mariners' Way**, an ancient path for sailors travelling from one Devon coast to the other to pick up their next boat. Easy walking brings us over a couple of streams to open land and an unfenced lane ahead (Wp.13 103M) where we turn right to **Aish**. We now have a gentle uphill stroll to the village and then downhill keeping left at the T-junction at **Forder** towards **Wonson**. Even though it's uphill, our step quickens as, if we've timed it correctly, the excellent pub at **Wonson** beckons, and a quick detour to the left at **Barrow Way Cross** (Wp.14 114M) brings us down to **The Northmore Arms**, one of our favourites.

Retracing our steps to the cross (and that slope seems a lot steeper now) we follow the road towards **Chagford** (left) and after 5 minutes come to **Providence** (Wp.15 123M), where we pick up blue waymarks for 'Coombe', turning right and negotiating a gate onto an earthy driveway past cottages.

The track gets rougher as we descend and soon, through a gate and across a brook, we turn left onto a pretty lane and almost immediately take a right fork to **Gidleigh** on an uphill track (Wp.16 133M). High hedges obscure the view, but soon arriving at a road, we turn left past the phone box and then right at **Gidleigh Cross** (Wp.17 142M) towards **Berrydown** and **Scorhill**. Just 100 yards up the road at some conifers, we pick up yellow waymarks for the **Mariners' Way** and take the broad gravel track to the left.

After 300 yards (Wp.18 147M) a junction offers three alternatives, and we take the middle way on a narrow path, still with yellow waymarks, into the trees ahead. We're not far from the well-known **Gidleigh Park Hotel** here, and we wander down on comfy pine needles turning right as we meet a track which brings us to a wooden footbridge across the **North Teign River** (Wp.19 155M). This is a great spot for a breather to admire the river, before a mercifully brief slog up through trees and along over a stile to a lane (Wp.20 161M). Now we're on the home stretch, turning right and crossing a cattle grid onto an ancient *drove road*. We pass the famous **Round Pound** (Wp.21 170M), a most substantial enclosure and *hut circle*, and after a brief step, rejoin our car by the trees at **Batworthy** (Wp.22 175M).

The dominance of **Cosdon Hill** (known also as **Cawsand Hill**) on Dartmoor's north-eastern edge qualified it as one of the old Beacon Hills used to signal major events, and the area is rich with evidence of habitation back into the Bronze Age, including the fascinating ancient sites of **Cosdon Row** (or **The Cemetery**) and **White Moor Stone Circle**. **South Zeal** is an interesting village which retains features such as the long narrow strips of land known as *burgage plots* dating back to medieval times, while the remains of the **Ramsley Copper Mine** bear witness to its industrial past.

Access by car:
Driving down the main street of **South Zeal** in a south-west direction the car park is clearly signed off to the right at the end of the street. Take care negotiating the speed bump at the entrance to the car park.

Leaving the car park (Wp.1 0M), we turn left and then reach **High Street** at a T-junction, then right to climb uphill out of the village past thatched cottages.

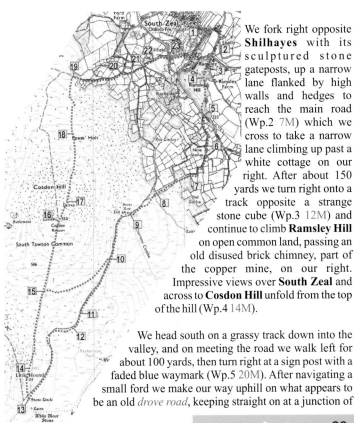

We fork right opposite **Shilhayes** with its sculptured stone gateposts, up a narrow lane flanked by high walls and hedges to reach the main road (Wp.2 7M) which we cross to take a narrow lane climbing up past a white cottage on our right. After about 150 yards we turn right onto a track opposite a strange stone cube (Wp.3 12M) and continue to climb **Ramsley Hill** on open common land, passing an old disused brick chimney, part of the copper mine, on our right. Impressive views over **South Zeal** and across to **Cosdon Hill** unfold from the top of the hill (Wp.4 14M).

We head south on a grassy track down into the valley, and on meeting the road we walk left for about 100 yards, then turn right at a sign post with a faded blue waymark (Wp.5 20M). After navigating a small ford we make our way uphill on what appears to be an old *drove road*, keeping straight on at a junction of tracks (Wp.6 25M) past an old wooden barn to our right. After a further 100 yards we follow the signposted track to the right between stone walls and climb steadily to a gate onto the moor (Wp.7 32M), rapidly gaining height on a broad corridor between boundary walls.

We strike out south-west from the corner of the wall on our right (Wp.8 41M), following an old peat cutters' path, clearly defined by a small depression making its way across the open moor.

The Cemetery

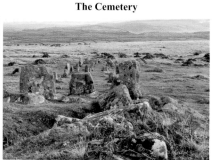

As we near the base of **Cosdon Hill** we come to **The Cemetery** (Wp.9 47M). These exceptionally well preserved Bronze Age remains include three parallel rows of stones processing up to three larger stones at the head, beyond which we find remains of a double *cist*, an ancient burial chamber.

Returning to the track we set off (SSW), now in a deep cutting between heather banks which climbs gently round the lower slopes of **Cosdon Hill** before levelling out (Wp.10 62M). To our left, the moor slopes away and becomes very boggy - it's a lonely spot and can be very exposed. Our path now veers right skirting around the marshy area known as **Raybarrow Pool**, the ground becoming progressively wetter. The track can become flooded after heavy rain, in which case follow the diversion.

Diversion (if Raybarrow Pool is impassable)

Retrace your steps back to Wp.10 and head south-west, climbing for 14 minutes onto the saddle between **Cosdon Hill** and **Little Hound Tor** to meet the return track at Wp.15. Either head south on the track to **White Moor Stone Circle** (Wp.13), or shorten the walk by heading north up **Cosdon Hill** (Wp.16).

White Moor Circle

Otherwise, and with great care, we seek out firm ground to take us across the wettest section (between Wp.11 72M and Wp.12 75M), then continue along the track in a shallow cutting around the side of **Little Hound Tor**, suddenly coming across **White Moor** stone circle dead ahead (Wp.13 98M).

Our return route takes us firstly over **Little Hound Tor** (Wp.14 103M N) and then on a steady climb up a well-trodden path to **Cosdon Beacon** (Wp.16 130M). It's like climbing on the back of an elephant, and the top is never in sight! Once we reach the trig point, we enjoy magnificent views north into central Devon, while an array of Dartmoor's highest peaks are on display to the south and west.

We head off along a peaty track past a large cairn (Wp.17 138M NNE) and on down towards **Sticklepath**. Soon we can see **South Zeal** to our right, noticing the medieval field strips which divide up the land. As we drop downhill, two stone posts lying across the track mark a fork in the path (Wp.18 150M) where we bear left in the direction of **Sticklepath**.

South Zeal

After a short left-right dog leg, we meet an old *drove road* (Wp.19 161M) and turn right, following the sunken stony track (E) to a gate leading off the moor (Wp.20 170M). Concrete replaces stone and we follow the signs for 'South Zeal'.

On reaching a junction, we follow the lane left (Wp.21 176M), then turn immediately right to go steeply down a narrow footpath and rejoin the lane (Wp.22 178M). We turn right down to the main road (Wp.23 180M) and go straight across heading for **South Zeal**.

At a T-junction we follow the road round left, turning left back into the car park (Wp.24 186M).

Refreshments are available in **South Zeal** High Street.

Foxtor Mires is said to have inspired the creation of the fictitious Grimpen Mire in the Hound of the Baskervilles and it's easy to understand why, if you visit this exposed and inhospitable area on a wet, foggy winter's day. In good weather, however, the area proves to be rich in ancient remains, explored on this walk as it skirts round the perimeter of the mire. After following **Devonport Leat** we contour round **Fox Tor** and **Ter Hill** before crossing the valley and walking round **Royal Hill**. On the way we visit **Goldsmith's Cross**, **Childe's Tomb** and **Crock of Gold Kistvaen** as well as old tin workings. A splendid day out - in good weather!

| 4/5 | 3¾ H | 9½ miles/15½km | 160m 160m | | 0 |

Access by car: From main crossroads in the centre of **Princetown**, turn down **Tor Royal Lane** between the **Wesleyan Chapel** and the **Foxtor Café**. Follow the lane round to the right and after 2 miles park on the right just past the driveway to **Peat Cot**.

From the car park (Wp.1 0M) we turn right on the lane strolling downhill towards the flat expanse of **Foxtor Mires**. A small stone bridge takes the lane over **Devonport Leat** (Wp.2 7M) and we turn sharp right on a small track along side the stream, starting the long circumnavigation of the mires on our left.

Foxtor Mires

A valley *mire* is an extensive area of soft, wet and spongy ground formed chiefly by rotting vegetation trapped in a badly drained valley. The areas are rich in a diverse range of plant, insect and animal life but great caution must be exercised when exploring such areas, as they contain deep bogs that reputedly claim the lives of animals that stray on to them. **Foxtor Mires** is such an area and while walking round this bleak, remote landscape it is easy to imagine the quaking, fog-shrouded scenes in Conan Doyle's book.

While wandering along, we notice various species of flora and fauna thriving in the *leat* that keep our interest, and there's an excellent sheep leap to be tested! (See the photo on the next page.)

Continuing, we follow the waterway as it swings right just below **Nun's Cross Farm**, contouring round the hillside past a track crossing and sluice gate (Wp.3 22M) to take a look as the *leat* disappears into a tunnel (Wp.4 24M). (Note: Walk 30 'Devonport Leat' visits the

The leat tunnel

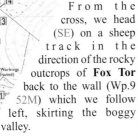

exit from the tunnel, about 800 yards west.)

Retracing our steps to the track crossing (Wp.3), we turn right, down to a stream and ford (improvised stepping stones on the left help us to cross keeping dry feet), climbing the bank and old tin workings on the other side. After 20 yards a small track left (Wp.5 27M) takes us alongside the workings to a stone wall (Wp.6 33M) which we cross and follow a worn track right (E).

We climb gently out of the valley, the wall on our right, then drop down to a stream. As we reach the brow of the small hill on the far side (Wp.7 43M) we leave the track turning left on heather and grass to **Goldsmith's Cross** 200 yards north (Wp.8 46M) named after Lieutenant Goldsmith who found the remains of the cross in 1903 and had it erected in its present position on top of a large rounded boulder overlooking the treacherous mire.

From the cross, we head (SE) on a sheep track in the direction of the rocky outcrops of **Fox Tor** back to the wall (Wp.9 52M) which we follow left, skirting the boggy valley.

Goldsmith's Cross and Foxtor Mires

Just 20 yards after the next small stream we leave the wall bearing left (NE) across rough grass to the substantial memorial cross known as **Childe's Tomb** (Wp.10 63M) from where we enjoy the wide open views across the bog.

We head east from the cross over spoils of tin mining to a large, distinct, rounded boulder (Wp.11 73M) in the middle of the **Swincombe Valley** which conveniently marks an excellent natural crossing point over the fast running stream.

Immediately over the stream, we turn left (N) towards the dilapidated walls of an old settlement and an obvious leaning stone post at one of the corners (Wp.12 78M).

Childe's Tomb

Childe's Tomb is said to be the place where the nobleman Childe of Plimstoke perished in the 11th century. Legend goes that after becoming separated from his companions during a hunting party, during severely cold weather, he killed his horse, disembowelling it and taking cover inside its body in an attempt to avoid exposure - to no avail as he was found later frozen to death. The present memorial was reconstructed in the 1880's as one of the first projects undertaken by the Dartmoor Preservation Society. The cross, over 7ft tall, sits on a granite block base constructed over a *cist*.

The leaning stone (Wp.12)

We continue (N) across rough, tumpy grass picking up after 20 yards the remains of an ancient wall and ditch which we follow using sheep tracks skirting round the lower slopes of **Ter Hill**. To our left **Foxtor Mires** appears lush and benign, sitting in a well-defined basin.

The ditch and wall intermittently vanish and reappear, and passing the start of a distinct wall on our left down to the mire (Wp.13 87M), we continue until we meet another stone wall running from **Ter Hill** down into the valley on our left (Wp.14 90M).

Crossing the wall we turn left following it down towards the **Swincombe River** until we meet the dry *leat* of **Wheal Emma** where we turn right (Wp.15 95M NE), onto a trodden path along the overgrown left hand bank. The river meanders along the valley below towards the reservoir at **Swincombe Intake Works** as we continue following the old watercourse until we're in line with the works entrance, next to two old stone gate posts in the wall on our right. (Wp.16 111M).

Turning left, we head downhill (NW) towards a large rock outcrop (Wp.17 113M), then on down to the gravel works access track (Wp.18 116M) where we turn right, and stroll on, enjoying the broad river valley as it winds through pasture land.

After ¾ mile we meet the **Dartmoor Way**, turning left to join it via a foot bridge over the river (Wp.19 127M). The broad stone path doubles as a stream for the first 100 yards but soon dries up as we climb keeping left, past the ruined remains of **Swincombe Farms** (W) reaching a gate with blue waymark leading onto the moor (Wp.20 137M).

Heading on the well-worn path directly towards the transmitter at **North Hessary** (WNW), our route stretches clearly ahead. We climb steadily uphill, then drop into a small valley, crossing a stream at **Cholake Head** (Wp.21 162M) and joining a broad stony track constructed during the war by conscientious objectors held at **Princetown**.

The Crock of Gold

After 500 yds we reach a large cairn on the right (Wp.22 169M) which acts as a marker for the particularly well preserved **Crock of Gold** *cist* (Wp.23 172M) found on the top of a small hillock 20 yards to the left of the track, one of several Bronze Age *cists* found on **Royal Hill**.

We continue on the track to a boundary at **Bull Park** where we turn left on a gravel path (SSE) alongside the wall on our right (Wp.24 184M). The path is clear and diverts in places around wet areas as we stride out on fairly level ground before dropping down into the **Strane River** valley using a foot bridge to cross the small stream (Wp.25 202M). Climbing the other side of the valley, we reach the stone retaining wall of the **Devonport Leat** and turn right through a waymarked gate(Wp.26 206M) towards **Peat Cot**. As we approach the house we turn left on the path crossing the *leat*, past a chapel, then climb gently uphill on an un-metalled track, reaching the road (Wp.27 219M) and turning left back to the carpark (Wp.28 222M).

This walk takes us first across open moor to the remarkable ancient stone rows at **Merrivale** and then, for a complete change of scenery, into the tranquil **Walkham Valley** - sheltered, calm and with an abundance of wild flowers. We admit to having a bit of a 'thing' about bluebells and on this walk in May they just get better and better. We then head for the tors following the track of the old **Plymouth and Dartmoor Railway** out into the wild, often bleak, granite landscape to explore a couple of disused quarries with so much evidence of their fascinating industrial history set out before us.

3	3¼ H	8 miles/13km	225m / 225m	3

Shortcut
To cut out the visit to **Foggintor Quarry**, follow the route to Wp.13. Turn left (NNE) on the small grassy track over to the car park at Wp.1 (2½ hours, 6½ miles/10km).

Access by car: On the B3357 Tavistock to Princetown road, park one mile east of **The Dartmoor Inn** at Merrivale on the south side of the road.

From the carpark (Wp.1 0M) we head away from the road (SW) towards **King's Tor** on the skyline and a large waymark stone in the near distance, from where (Wp.2 3M), we can pick out the letters 'T' and 'A', standing for **Tavistock** and **Ashburton**; this stone (amongst others) indicated the route across the moor for travellers in times past. We continue (W) to a second and then a third waymark stone, coming to the terminus of the first of two double stone rows - we've arrived at the famous **Merrivale** antiquities (Wp.3 9M).

Merrivale

With its wealth of impressive monuments dating back at least 4000 years, **Merrivale** was a place of great ritual significance for Bronze Age settlers. The largest and most varied of such prehistoric sites on Dartmoor, it consists of three stone rows, a stone circle, standing stones, several cairns and *cists*. Two of the stone rows are double and almost parallel, each with single large blocking stones at the eastern end, unique on Dartmoor. A cairn circle containing a *cist* (somewhat difficult to locate) is halfway along the southern row, and just to the south of the rows is a fine *kistvaen* (cist), sadly with its cover stone missing. The *menhir* or standing stone rises 10½ feet above ground level - magnificent!

Leaving the heart of this evocative site, we set off (SW) towards the large *menhir*, standing close to a wall with the trees of the **Walkham Valley** behind, to find that this imposing stone is accompanied by an obvious stone circle (Wp.4 18M). Our route now takes us towards the **Merrivale** quarries visible

Vixen Tor

ahead and we bear right, skirting the wall until we descend to the road (Wp.5 27M) and turn left for 100 yards to a farm (Wp.6 28M). **The Dartmoor Inn** nestles below on the right, a possible refreshment stop. The signed bridlepath to the left takes us through a metal gate onto a stony track in unfenced farmland; as we climb gently we catch sight of **Vixen Tor** to the right - a real challenge for climbers.

Lush banks of bluebells

We stroll past the house at **Longash** where our track dwindles to a grassy path and meander in and out of woodland on a pretty route through tranquil countryside. This refreshing stretch soon brings us down to a set of three gates at **Daveytown** (Wp.7 55M) where we carry straight on, now on a metalled lane with a drift of gorgeous wild flowers alongside us in lush banks - the bluebells here in May are just stunning.

We pass by **Withill** (an idyllic spot for a B&B) and soon come to **Criptor Cross** (Wp.8 75M) where we turn left towards **Criptor**.

The disused railway track

The road peters out over the cattle grid and at a track junction (Wp.9 81M) we turn right alongside a boundary wall for about 150 yards and as the track turns right we continue on a grassy path (SE) heading for **Ingra Tor**. We soon pick up a disused railway track (Wp.10 86M) and follow it to the left around the base of the tor passing quarrying remains as we head out into wild open countryside - what a contrast to that beautiful secluded valley earlier in our walk. It's easy walking now on this clear track and, passing much evidence of the old railway, we make good progress around to **Swelltor Quarries**.

Turning off to the right (Wp.11 119M) we scramble up to the main workings as they become accessible. It's worth spending a few minutes here exploring this abandoned industrial site - but some of the cut granite blocks do make very handy picnic tables!

We keep to the higher track heading onwards (NW) past the *corbels* (Wp.12 130M) and soon rejoin our previous rail track, its raised green curve disappearing round the back of **King's Tor** to our right. Soon coming to the north side of the tor (Wp.13 142M) we can see our carpark directly ahead just

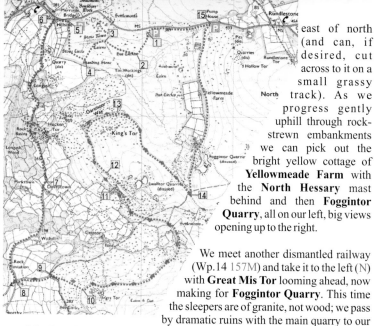

east of north (and can, if desired, cut across to it on a small grassy track). As we progress gently uphill through rock-strewn embankments we can pick out the bright yellow cottage of **Yellowmeade Farm** with the **North Hessary** mast behind and then **Foggintor Quarry**, all on our left, big views opening up to the right.

We meet another dismantled railway (Wp.14 157M) and take it to the left (N) with **Great Mis Tor** looming ahead, now making for **Foggintor Quarry**. This time the sleepers are of granite, not wood; we pass by dramatic ruins with the main quarry to our right (worth an explore if time allows) heading for the vivid buildings of **Yellowmeade Farm**. We step out again, still on the main track contouring the hillside and passing an interesting area of enclosures on the left as we approach the road. A bridge takes us across a small stream at the junction (Wp.15 185M) and we turn left using the grassy verge for safety as we head back to our car (Wp.16 195M).

Railways and Quarries

In the early 1800s Sir Thomas Tyrwhitt had a vision for Dartmoor which included the construction of a horse drawn tramway to link **Plymouth** with **Princetown**. This would allow granite, a valuable building material, to be 'exported' from the moor whilst lime, coal and other necessities could be brought in for the community to soften this unforgiving land. The scheme was not a great success but later, in the steam age, the track was re-laid and levelled, some of the more acute bends being taken out (but still visible on our walk). GWR eventually took over the line, finally closed in 1956 having never been a commercial success.

However, the considerable evidence of activity at **Swelltor** and **Foggintor** quarries indicates that great quantities of fine quality granite were extracted; some was reputed to be used for Nelson's column and more was destined for London Bridge - take a look at the twelve *corbels* at Wp.12 that never made it to London.

A quick scan of the map reveals why this most westerly peninsula of the **Dartmoor National Park** is so attractive. It has steeply wooded valleys, the meeting of two rivers and good open views from the tops, - an ideal place for a short afternoon walk. We start at the pretty **Grenofen Bridge** and follow the **Walkham River** to its meeting point with the **Tavy**, then strike out uphill to Dartmoor's most westerly tor. We return across the moor with expansive views of Dartmoor on the skyline before dropping back down to the river and returning to the car.

1 | 2H | 5 miles/8km | 140m / 140m | 0

Access by car: On the A386 travelling north from **Horrabridge**, turn left opposite **The Halfway House Inn** (1½ miles after the **River Walkham** crossing at **Bedford Bridge**). After 100 yards, take the first left down to **Grenofen Bridge** and park on the right.

Shortcut
Follow the route to Wp.13 and turn left down the hill back to **Grenofen Bridge** (1½ hours, 4miles/6km)

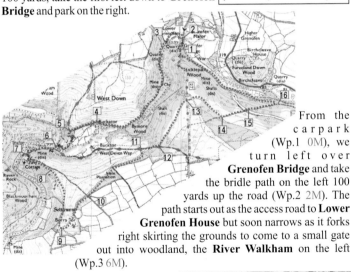

From the car park (Wp.1 0M), we turn left over **Grenofen Bridge** and take the bridle path on the left 100 yards up the road (Wp.2 2M). The path starts out as the access road to **Lower Grenofen House** but soon narrows as it forks right skirting the grounds to come to a small gate out into woodland, the **River Walkham** on the left (Wp.3 6M).

Ignoring a track to the right, we follow the river through this deeply wooded valley, coming across evidence of past mining activity typified by a handsome, sturdy stone chimney. The river on our left meanders gently through tranquil pools, then rushes and tumbles over waterfalls and rapids before we fork right climbing up to **Buckator House** (Wp.4 24M), turning left on a broad gravel track

The River Walkham

with the house on our left. At a T-junction (Wp.5 28M) we bear left tacking down the steep hill and passing **Watersmeet Cottage** on the left, back towards the **River Walkham**.

Double Waters

In 300 yards we're confronted by a rock face past which the river squeezes on the left, but we climb right, through a small cleft and 'Hey Presto', we emerge into the somewhat grander **Tavy River** valley; we bear left to **Double Waters**, a small triangle of land at the confluence of the rivers (Wp.6 33M). A robust wooden bridge takes us across the **Walkham** where we follow a track to the right, climbing steadily and leaving the river.

At a block-work outbuilding (Wp.7 39M) we turn left to follow the path as it climbs quite steeply through trees, then come into a more open grassy area from where we enjoy stunning views to the south down the wooded **Tavy** valley. Leaving the track after 350 yards (Wp.8 45M), we turn right following a well used grassy path which skirts around the hillside just above the tree line. A gentle climb and left turn (NE) brings us to **Berra Tor** (Wp.9 56M), the most westerly tor on Dartmoor - gorgeous views and a fine place to lazy about on a sunny day!

The posts after Wp.10

We follow the path along the hilltop, passing left of a copse and crossing a track (Wp.10 63M), going straight ahead between two posts through well-grazed moorland left and trees right, high Dartmoor tors on the skyline. Gradually descending, the path becomes stony and swings left towards a metalled lane below where we turn right (Wp.11 75M) passing through a small wooded dip. Emerging from the trees we head left on a grassy track (Wp.12 78M). Ambling along, we climb gently across well-cropped pasture (NNE), enjoying views into the **Walkham** valley and beyond, then cross a well-used track (Wp.13 85M). (N.B. Turn left on the track to return to the carpark at **Grenofen Bridge**).

Following the main track as it gradually swings right through 90 degrees, we head south-east contouring round the hillside. At a cross tracks (Wp.14 91M) we turn left on a narrow path downhill into trees, soon crossing a bridge over a deep cutting made for the **Yelverton** to **Tavistock** railway (Wp.15 95M) then immediately bear right downhill. On reaching a well-used track (Wp.16 99M), we turn acutely left back on ourselves soon catching glimpses of the river through the trees. Keeping to the track we walk alongside this lovely babbling river hoping to spot a solitary kingfisher or dipper before we arrive back at our car (Wp.17 115M).

The **Drizzlecombe Stone Rows** are one of Dartmoor's most famous antiquities. This walk takes us right into the heart of this site after a lovely moorland climb passing **Crazy Well Pool** and the reknowned **Siward's Cross** on the way. But - even better - we get the intricate **Yellowmead** stone circles thrown in for good measure as we return, followed by a relaxing woodland stroll back to the car.

4	3½ H	9½ miles/15km	260m / 260m	↻	0

Access by car: On the B3212 from **Yelverton** towards **Princetown** turn right at **The Burrator Inn**, **Dousland**. After ¾ mile fork left towards the reservoir and then right at the dam, keeping the water on the left. Turn left after ½ mile and then follow the road around the reservoir for 1½ miles to **Norsworthy Bridge** and park.

> This walk can be mixed and matched at Wp.9 with Walk 30 at Wp.15

Facing **Norsworthy Bridge** with the reservoir to our left (Wp.1 0M), we take the right turn, waymarked with a selection of paw prints, on a broad stony track uphill into trees. As the path splits after 100 yards (Wp.2 2M), we fork left into **Norsworthy Plantation** on a public bridleway and, ignoring occasional stiles into the woodland on either side, meander upwards with the pretty **Meavy River** valley below on our left.

Arriving at **Leather Tor Bridge** (Wp.3 9M) our way to 'Older Bridge and Peat Cot' appears to be a scramble up the bank to our right but in fact, we continue straight ahead for 50 yards and then take the right fork leading us away from the river.

The cross near Crazy Well Pool

We wind our way gently up the hill into conifers to a T-junction (Wp.4 16M) where we make a right followed by a quick left turn and head out towards open countryside.

A gateway takes us onto the moor (Wp.5 23M) and, continuing straight ahead on the broad track, across a small stream which we follow up to the left on a small diversion to **Crazy Well Pool** (Wp.6 32M); not a natural pool, it was made by the medieval tinners who worked much of this area. Gruesome legends abound of its ability to foretell death!

Making for our original path (SE), we take in a restored cross on the way, then stroll on lightly trodden grass (E), soon rejoining the broader stony track (Wp.7 36M).

Stepping out in this glorious open moorland, we admire another cross to the right then meet the **Devonport Leat** as it comes in from the left at **Older Bridge** (Wp.8 52M).

Turning right, we follow the watercourse on a small grassy path, contouring round the hillside and enjoying gorgeous views down **Newleycombe Lake**. Just past a small, square concrete building, we cross over to the left hand side of the water and soon see where the *leat* emerges from the hill via a tunnel (Wp.9 69M), and if you're wondering where the entrance is, see Walk 26.

Nun's Cross

Continuing east on the line of the hidden waterway, clambering over the mounds and dips of the old tin workings, we come to the top and the magnificent **Siward's Cross** appears ahead (Wp.10 73M). Also known as **Nun's Cross** and dating from at least 1240, it stands at just over 2 metres and is surely one of the most impressive of its kind on Dartmoor.

Turning right (S) on the wide sandy track, we soon spot the *leat* again down past **Nun's Cross Farm** below on the left and as we gain height the treacherous wastes of **Foxtor Mires** come into sight, rendered infamous in The Hound of the Baskervilles as 'Grimpen Mire'; not one of Dartmoor's friendlier locations. We trudge on gently up into the bald moorland hills, keeping to the right as the track splits near the top of our climb (Wp.11 92M) where we pass more tin workings, a fenced off mine shaft to the right (Wp.12 99M) and remains of old buildings either side.

Good views unfold before us as we start to make our way downhill, passing a fern clad ruined wall to our left, then forking left off the main track on a broad level grassy path (Wp.13 108M), quickly reaching a cross-tracks (Wp.14 110M). We go left, the ruins of a smelting house on our right, down to a ford which we cross and then turn right (S) on a grassy path parallel to the stream. Now we have our first glimpse of the spectacular *menhirs* of the **Drizzlecombe Stone Rows** ahead and right.

After 500 yards (Wp.15 116M) we strike off slightly left and uphill (SE) on a narrow path, admiring stone circles on our right until we come to a track in line with the *menhirs* (Wp.16 120M). Looking down, we get a real sense of the grandeur and scale of the site, then turning right for a much closer look. (See the photo and background notes below.)

We wander along the stone row to the first large standing stone (Wp.17 130M) and possibly investigate **Giant's Basin** a few yards ahead to its left before wandering down the second row to its own massive *menhir* (Wp.18 133M).

Continuing (SW) we cross **Drizzlecombe Brook** at stepping stones (Wp.19 139M), our track broadening as we head gradually uphill - it's really worth turning round here to view the impressive stone rows from this angle. Following the line of the **River Plym**, we arrive at **Ditsworthy Warren House** (Wp.20 148M), deserted now but occasionally used for training by the MOD, the *pillow mounds* nearby a reminder of when it served as a warren farm for breeding rabbits.

Drizzlecombe Stone Rows

These prehistoric remains (probably dating from between the end of the Neolithic to the Early Bronze Age, 2500-1500 BC), consist mainly of three stone rows and one enormous cairn.

The tallest *menhir*

Each row is oriented south-west to north-east with a cairn at the upper end and a *menhir* at the lower, the two rows we walk being the most obvious. The third row is to the right and is built from smaller stones, its *menhir* standing at 2.4m while our first *menhir* is an impressive 4.3m (the tallest on Dartmoor) and the second still imposing at 3.2m. The small 'hill' to the left of the start of the lower row is actually the huge cairn of **Giant's Basin**. It has three tiny cairns on its west side and a dip in the top - hence, 'Basin'.

This must be one of the finest such sites on Dartmoor, the true purpose of which intriguingly still remains unknown.

We bear right (NW) to pick up **Edward's Path** which leads us alongside **Gutter Mire** towards a small stand of conifers and through a gate to a scout hut (Wp.21 167M). Here we turn right on a stony track for 100 yards until we're in line with the end of the conifers (Wp.22 169M).

Yellowmead stone circles

We cross a waterway and follow it to the left (N) on a grassy track, then swing left (NW) making for the pointed boundary stone ahead (Wp.23 176M). The great granite outcrop of **Sheeps Tor** guides us to the four concentric stone circles at **Yellowmead** (Wp.24 183M), seemingly a popular spot for sheep.

The clear grassy path (N) skirts an area of gorse to the left. Forking left down to a dip, we track the wall on our left up to stepping stones over a *leat* (Wp.25 191M) and head in the direction of the pyramidal summit of **Leather Tor** (NNW). We drop down the east side of **Sheeps Tor** to a wall that encloses trees (Wp.26 197M) and take the track to the left off the moor and down to the road (Wp.27 205M) where we turn right back to our car (Wp.28 212M).

The *leats* of Dartmoor are remarkable features providing plenty of interest and easy walking access to remote moorland. This walk takes advantage of one of the most remarkable of these waterways, the **Devonport Leat**, followings its path from **Burrator Reservoir** up to its disappearance into a tunnel just south of **Nun's Cross**. On our return to the reservoir we discover the impressive **Down Tor** stone row - in our view one of the best to be seen - before strolling back down to **Norsworthy Bridge**.

| 3 | 3H | 7½ miles/12km | 200m / 200m | ↻ | 0 |

Access by car: On the B3212 from **Yelverton** towards **Princetown**, turn right at **The Burrator Inn**, **Dousland**. After ¾ mile, fork left towards the reservoir, then right at the dam, keeping the water on the left. Turn left after ½mile and follow the road around the reservoir for 1½ miles to **Norsworthy Bridge** and park.

Variation
This walk can be mixed and matched at Wp.15 with Walk 29 at Wp.9.

We leave the car park (Wp.1 0M) at **Norsworthy Bridge** at the head of **Burrator Reservoir**. Walking anticlockwise round the reservoir, we cross the bridge and turn immediately right over a stile onto a footpath signed 'Devonport Leat' (Wp.2 2M).

We follow the path as it winds its way uphill through mixed woodland. After crossing a stony track and scrambling up the bank of the *leat* (Wp.3 9M) we turn right along the side of this two hundred year old waterway, walking through the **Stanlake Plantation** against the flow of the stream which bubbles along on our left. The gravel path makes easy walking, allowing plenty of opportunities to spot fish darting through the crystal clear water. As we reach the edge of the plantation (Wp.4 25M) a stile takes us onto the moorland, and we continue along the side of the *leat* past the remains of an old settlement on our left with the **River Meavy** in the valley below. After a kilometre, at (Wp.5 35M), we cross to the left hand side, just before the channel swings sharply right. We are

Devonport Leat was built in the 1790s to supply water to the **Devonport** docks in **Plymouth** but it now terminates at **Burrator Reservoir**. It is one of the most impressive of Dartmoor's *leats*, being fed by the **West Dart**, **Cowsic** and **Blackbrook** rivers from its head just north of **Wistman's Wood**. It has many interesting features - aqueducts, a tunnel and even a waterfall as it descends into the **Meavy River** at **Raddick Hill**. One marvels at the skill and effort required in constructing such a waterway!

confronted by water tumbling down the side of **Raddick Hill** onto an aqueduct across the **Meavy River**(Wp.6 36M). Quite a spectacular sight!

(N.B. The following diversion can be cut out by crossing the aqueduct and following the *leat* to Wp.12 up the hill)

Black Tor Hole

From the aqueduct we take a diversion from the *leat* to explore old tin workings and the **Black Tor** logan stone. We follow an exposed metal pipe (NE) up the **Meavy Valley**. Staying on the river's left bank, we clamber over old tin workings and arrive at **Black Tor Hole** (Wp.7 44M), a small plunge pool at the foot of an impressive cascade.

The ruins of two old *Blowing Houses* used until the mid-17th century are found on the pool's edge, each containing mortar stones.

Blowing houses were water powered smelting mills where tin ore, extracted from alluvial deposits, was crushed and ground on mortar stones by a stamping machine before being melted on a bed of charcoal in a forced draught furnace. The resulting tin ingots were taken to one of the four local *stannary* towns of **Ashburton**, **Chagford**, **Plympton** or **Tavistock** for assaying.

Black Tor logan stone

From **Black Tor Pool** we head NW, climbing up to **Black Tor** (Wp.8 52M) with its two rock outcrops, the smaller bearing a huge logan stone which until recently could be rocked from side to side.

Instead of retracing our steps to the aqueduct we head back downhill (SE) to **Black Tor Ford** (Wp.9 57M) across the **Meavy**, just upstream from the waterfall visited earlier. A small improvised metal bridge takes us across and we bear left, negotiating some wet ground and heading for a stone row on the hillside (Wp.10 60M) from where we pick up a rough track heading south to **Hart Tor Brook**. We turn left, following the fast flowing water upstream until we find a second welcome metal bridge, making for an easy crossing (Wp.11 65M).

Now we contour round **Raddick Hill** to the right (SW), using a rough grassy track until we meet the *leat* again (Wp.12 70M), this time at the top of its steep descent to the aqueduct in the valley below. Heading uphill, we follow a track alongside the *leat* as it carves its way through the bilberry and bracken covered moor. The views are stunning, the wooded surroundings of **Burrator Reservoir** on our right in extreme contrast to the desolate **Cramber Tor** moorland to the left. The *leat* cuts across spoils of old mine workings, heading up the **Newleycombe Lake** valley and we converge with a track on our right which gradually climbs from the valley and intersects the *leat* (Wp.13 110M). We continue following the channel round the head of the valley, passing a small concrete shed and a cross up on the left (Wp.14 118M) until it eventually disappears into a tunnel through the hill (Wp.15 124M).

Variation:
This walk can be mixed and matched at Wp.15 with Walk 29 at Wp.9.

We leave the *leat*, heading (SW)across fairly flat terrain and picking up a well-defined grassy track that goes directly towards the sheer face of **Sheeps Tor** , visible on the skyline.

The stone circle

We make for a cairn (Wp.16 141M) and stone circle from where we can see, directly ahead, a remarkable stone row - one of the best on Dartmoor. We head for the terminal stone (Wp.17 144M), then walk following the row, counting 154 stones culminating in a magnificent 2.5 metre *menhir* (Wp.18 150M) and a well preserved stone circle. Not to be missed!

From the circle we bear right heading west to **Down Tor**, and as we approach it (Wp.19 160M), views of **Burrator Reservoir** and the hills on the other side open up. We continue west, heading down to an outcrop of rocks in line with the end of the reservoir (Wp.20 170M) then picking up a well-trodden path to continue our descent.

After passing through a boundary wall, we head on down to the car park at **Norsworthy Bridge** (Wp.1 177M).

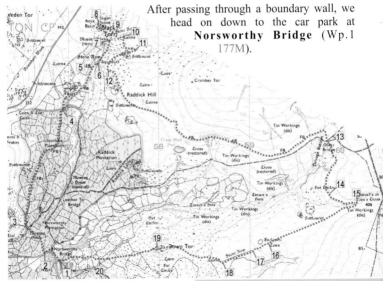

No apologies are made for including this very popular walk which circumnavigates the spectacular valley carved out by the river Plym as it cascades down from the moor. This picturesque valley is a major recreational area for walking and rock climbing and has a rich industrial history with many relics of past activity to be seen. We start with a moderate climb, then following the well known "Pipe Track" we stroll up the valley to **Cadover Bridge** returning on the opposite side over **Dewerstone Rocks**, finally descending via the old tramway.

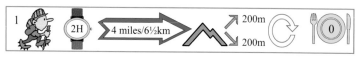

Access by car: From the A386 **Plymouth** to **Tavistock** road, turn at **Roborough** towards **Bickleigh** and **Shaugh Prior**. Carry on straight through **Bickleigh** turning left after the army camp to **Shaugh Prior**. After 1.5 miles, immediately over **Shaugh Bridge**, park in the carpark on the left.

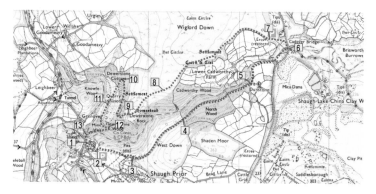

From **Shaugh Bridge** carpark (Wp.1 0M) our path follows signs to **Cadover Bridge** up steep steps alongside old china clay drying kilns, turning right towards the road and then left, striking off uphill into mixed woodland. Straight ahead over a stile (Wp.2 4M) we make our way around boulders, still climbing quite steeply up the valley side.

As we reach the crest of the hill, we briefly emerge from the woodland to our first glimpse of the impressive **Dewerstone Rocks** on our left across the valley. The path climbs more gently now as we follow the old pipeline used to bring china clay from the quarry at the head of the valley down to **Shaugh Bridge**. After passing near a house on the right we reach a gate (Wp.3 17M) and continue following the well trodden path alongside the pipeline back into the woods. The views of **Dewerstone Rocks** are particularly good from here especially during winter months through the leafless trees.

At the next stile (Wp.4 29M) we enter **North Wood** (NT) to wander along the level path with the rushing sounds from the river below growing ever louder as we progress up the valley.

The pipe track at Wp.5

Negotiating a small wooden bridge and stile (Wp.5 42M) we exit **North Wood** into a small paddock and after a brief climb clamber over a ladder stile back into woodland. After 400 yards we arrive at an open grassy area alongside the river at the head of the valley and make for **Cadover Bridge** clearly visible ahead.

From **Cadover Bridge** (Wp.6 50M) we see the earth *bunds* surrounding the still very active china clay quarry and the **River Plym** meandering through a marshy plain from the distant open moor. We stroll over the bridge to turn left on a grassy track through gorse heading (W) towards the stone cross on the hill ahead (Wp.7 54M) and, as we gain height, the clay works behind us become even more prominent. Leaving the cross we head on to the open moorland of **Wigford Down** following the boundary wall on our left (NW then SW) on a well-trodden path. A large outcrop of rocks (Wp.8 74M) provides an excellent vantage point for the sheer rock faces of the **Dewerstone** and allows us to reflect on the **Dewerstone** legend.

Dewerstone Rocks

The precipitous cliffs on the north eastern side of the **Plym Valley**, known as **Dewerstone Rocks**, were named according to ancient legend through their association with the Devil (Dewer being an old name for the Devil). The legend which also inspired Sir Arthur Conan Doyle to write the Hound of the Baskervilles speaks of the "Hounds of Hell" driven on by the Devil chasing benighted travellers to the Rocks where they would fall the 120 feet to their death. Not many folk have seen the Devil or his Hounds recently, but frequently people can be seen descending from the rocks on ropes!

We soon come to the tor (Wp.9 81M) above **Dewerstone Rocks** from which, on a clear day, we have fine views to **Plymouth** (S) and the higher Dartmoor tors (NE). We begin our descent (W) into woods, climbing over a boundary wall and then swinging right (N) past several old quarry workings to a derelict building, once the cable brake drum house for a 19th century inclined tramway (Wp.10 91M). We double back on ourselves following the steady descent of the tramway, carrying straight on at a junction (Wp.11 100M) and then climbing slightly to a left bend round a rocky outcrop. The path descends towards the **Plym** valley, keeping right at a split (Wp.12 105M) and zigzagging down to river level. With the river on our left, we stroll along the broad path to cross **Shaugh Bridge** via a small wooden footbridge, leading back to the carpark (Wp.13 113M).

The land around **Burrator Reservoir** is particularly attractive as it offers such variety. This walk takes us first up onto the high moor with tremendous views and then from this exposed spot we meander down through woods and farmland to pretty Dartmoor villages. We come upon some handsome crosses, a beautiful church and a welcoming pub before heading again to higher territory, a *leat* finally guiding us back to the start through yet more tranquil woodland.

Access by car: On the B3212 from **Yelverton** towards **Princetown**, turn right at **The Burrator Inn, Dousland**. After ¾ mile, fork left towards the reservoir and then right at the dam, keeping the water on your left. Turn left after ½ mile, then follow the road around the reservoir for 2 miles to **Norsworthy Bridge** and park.

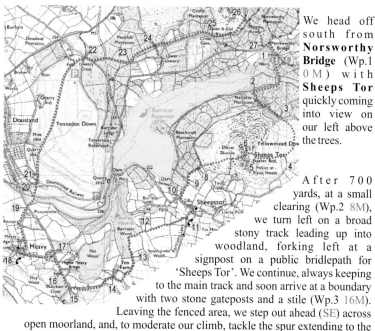

We head off south from **Norsworthy Bridge** (Wp.1 0 M) w i t h **Sheeps Tor** quickly coming into view on our left above the trees.

After 700 yards, at a small clearing (Wp.2 8M), we turn left on a broad stony track leading up into woodland, forking left at a signpost on a public bridlepath for 'Sheeps Tor'. We continue, always keeping to the main track and soon arrive at a boundary with two stone gateposts and a stile (Wp.3 16M). Leaving the fenced area, we step out ahead (SE) across open moorland, and, to moderate our climb, tackle the spur extending to the east of **Sheeps Tor**. As we head for the rocky outcrop at the top we swing to the right (W) along the spur, the views open up, and we pass first one cut granite stone (Wp.4 27M), and then a second (Wp.5 35M) before climbing up to the tor itself (Wp.6 38M). As we stroll around the summit enjoying the landscape before us we can pick out **Burrator Reservoir**, the pointed crags of **Leather Tor** (N) with **Sharpitor** behind, the television mast at **North Hessary** and an expanse of tors around to the east. It is said that the pixies have a house in one of the many clefts and cracks associated with **Sheeps Tor** - but in our experience, they seem to like to keep themselves well hidden.

We begin our descent (SW) carefully picking our way through boulders to a worn grassy path making for a third stone marker (Wp.7 42M) and then heading for the leftmost point of the reservoir to trees ahead and a wooden gate in a stone wall (Wp.8 48M). Leaving the moor down a stony corridor, we quickly come to a lane and turn left (Wp.9 50M) passing 'Byeways' on our right as we approach a T-junction (Wp.10 54M), there taking a left towards **Sheepstor**. A fine cross welcomes us to the village with its pretty church behind, itself having another interesting cross built into the stile leading to what was the playing field - worth exploring if time permits.

We turn right in **Sheepstor** along a small lane, cross **Sheepstor Brook** and, as the lane starts to climb, almost immediately come to a gate on the right signed as a public footpath to 'Marchant's Cross' (Wp11 57M). Following the path with yellow waymarks guiding us, we wiggle round the side of some barns, bear left diagonally across a field to a metal gate, then follow the wall on the right to a large beech tree set in the corner of the field.

Sheepstor Church has a famous connection with India, being the resting place of Sir James Brooke, Rajah of Sarawak. Sir James was born in Bengal and on retirement made his home at **Burrator House** nearby. He died in 1868 and was buried in **Sheepstor** graveyard in a massive tomb of Aberdeen granite - a strange extravagance given the abundance of granite locally.

Intriguing stone steps built into a stile (Wp.12 65M) take us along a short stretch and then a wooden stile carries us over into pretty woodland for a lovely winding downhill ramble, occasional yellow dots on trees reminding us of our way. We exit the wood to the left over tree roots and a stile (Wp.13 71M), our path veering right and downhill through a metal gate and on quickly to a set of four gates - and here we bear left over a wooden stile still following the yellow waymarks.

Stepping stones over the Meavy

Skirting fields and into a little woodland valley we come down to the road at **Yeo Farm** (Wp.14 79M) and turn left along the quiet, undulating lane through charming countryside. A six minute stroll brings us to **Marchant's Cross** (Wp.15 84M) where we turn right down to the **River Meavy**, negotiating it via stepping stones (Wp.16 86M) - or maybe by the road bridge to the right for the fainthearted! We stay on the lane until we meet the **Yelverton** road (Wp.17 90M) and turn left alongside the primary school into **Meavy** with its village green complete with the **Meavy Oak** and the pub - **The Royal Oak Inn**, ideal for a refreshment stop. Our route is a sharp right just before the green (Wp.18 94M) and leaving the village behind, we walk uphill between high banks clad with an abundance of luscious growth to a T-junction (Wp.19 101M). We go straight across through the wooden gate opposite, fork left up onto the bank ahead and cross a second road (Wp.20 105M) heading onto gorse clad **Yennadon Down**.

We're on a public footpath which takes us across a dismantled railway to a bridge over a dried up *leat* (Wp.21 108M) where we fork left on the narrower track gently uphill, always keeping to the left of the highest point on **Yennadon Down**. We continue (NNE), following the main track (which can be unclear at times) and, as we climb, the terrain becomes more exposed and we have good views to the south and west. Our path levels and we step out briskly, the **North Hessary** mast directly ahead, making for trees and a car park which appear to our right (Wp.22 125M). We turn right at the road and then immediately left on a smaller metalled lane leading downhill and after five minutes come to a public footpath crossing us (Wp.23 131M).

Marchant's Cross, probably a corruption of 'merchant' is Dartmoor's tallest wayside cross marking an ancient path running between **Tavistock Abbey** and **Plympton Priory**; the **Abbot's Way**. As with many of Dartmoor's landmarks, legends abound. It's said that the cross marks the burial place of a suicide sited out of the village at crossroads in order to confuse evil spirits.

Cross Gate

Here we climb steps to the left and over a stile into woodland with the **Devonport** *leat* running below on the right, soon coming out of the trees onto moorland at a gate and stile (Wp.24 136M). Ignoring a turning to the right, we keep straight ahead, walking parallel with the road on a grassy path through woods and fields. Joining the road, we walk alongside the *leat* until we reach **Cross Gate** (Wp.25 145M).

The road bears right but we continue with the *leat* and, negotiating a stile at **Burrator Cross**, follow it going straight on over a stony track and past a small rectangular concrete building. About 200 yards further on we turn right, away from the water course, down to a broken signpost (Wp.26 152M) and head downhill on a narrow path crossing a broad stony track and coming to a stile. We continue over the stile into pretty woodland (occasionally frequented by deer) and stroll down to a road (Wp.27 158M) where we turn left over **Norsworthy Bridge** to rejoin our car (Wp.28 160M).

This walk explores the most southerly point of Dartmoor and gives us wonderful, expansive views across to the south Devon coast whilst picking up a bit of history on the way. It's not too strenuous an excursion as we stroll over the rounded hills, making progress to our high points at **Ugborough** and **Western Beacons** before returning to our car via an old dismantled tramway known as 'Puffing Billy'.

Access by car: From the A38 turn off to **Ivybridge** on the B3213 towards the town centre. Turn right at the roundabout by the Methodist Church and continue straight across the next roundabout to **Bittaford** and **Ugborough**. At **The Bridge Inn** turn right towards **Harford** and at the next mini-roundabout turn left, again to **Harford**. After ½ mile turn right at **Stowford Bridge** and follow the road to **Harford**, turning right at the church. Park through the gate ½ mile up the lane.

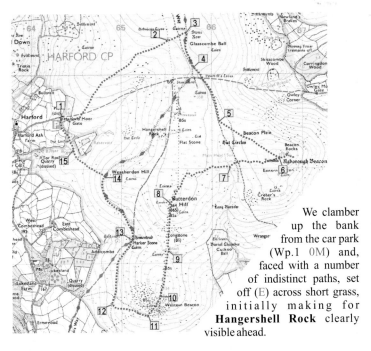

We clamber up the bank from the car park (Wp.1 0M) and, faced with a number of indistinct paths, set off (E) across short grass, initially making for **Hangershell Rock** clearly visible ahead.

After 3 minutes we start to swing left (NE), running parallel with the valley lying below to our right on a gentle uphill. Our track splits and divides but we keep to our bearing, aiming for the head of the valley to reach a boundary stone on an obvious track, more stones leading away up **Piles Hill** to our left (Wp.2 23M).

Keeping straight ahead, we very quickly reach a broad track - the dismantled **Ivybridge** to **Red Lake** tramway, used until the mid-30s to support the china clay quarries further north in the moor (Wp.3 27M).

Spurrell's Cross

We turn right, enjoying the views that begin to open up, and after 400 yards, where the tramway veers to the right, fork left on a grassy path (Wp.4 31M) with **Spurrell's Cross** in our sights. This sturdy, rough hewn cross has been restored and its site affords great views over to the east to **South Brent** and way beyond, but we carry on (SSE) until our track splits again (Wp.5 40M).

Ugborough Beacon

Here we leave the main grassy path to head uphill (SE) to the rocks above and soon reach the summit of **Ugborough Beacon** (Wp.6 50M) from where the view is superb.

Having explored the various peaks and crags, we make for **Butterdon Hill** (W), distinguished by its two flattish rock piles. To maintain height, we head just to the right of the hilltop using rough tracks through the grass - if only the sheep would always decide to go our way - a pleasant little green dip by **Lud Brook** (Wp.7 62M) forming a sheltered resting place. A gradual ascent brings us to the brow of the hill and we keep left, coming first to cairns and then to the trig point at the top of **Butterdon Hill** (Wp.8 76M). The views are again spectacular - **Hangershell Rock** with moorland behind to the north, clay quarries over to the west, a patchwork of fields to the east and south, with the coast in the distance and last but not least, a clear path to our next hilltop, **Western Beacon** (S).

We step out past **Black Pool** (Wp.9 84M) with the wooded **Erme Valley** below to our right, following the line of the boundary stones taking us up **Western Beacon**. The summit (Wp.10 91M) is the most southerly peak on the moor - and, yes, there are outstanding views! A large, obvious boundary stone can be found which is clearly inscribed 'U' (**Ugborough**) and 'H' (**Harford**) and is just one of the numerous stones marking this land division. It is believed that many of these stones may have been taken from the **Butterdon Hill Stone Row** which originally ran for just over a mile towards **Piles Hill**.

Leaving this somewhat exposed spot, we can see our track running round the base of the hill with **Ivybridge** sprawling behind; we make our way downhill

(SW) towards it, turning right as we meet it (Wp.11 96M). We drop gently down towards the woods of the **Erme Valley** (W) and, on meeting the tramway again, turn right (Wp.12 102M) now on the home stretch. This is easy walking - we pass a marker stone where the **Two Moors Way** joins us (Wp.13 111M) and after a further ten minutes of contouring around **Butterdon** and **Weatherdon Hills**, we strike off left towards a small conifer plantation.

By Butter Brook

The small grassy path immediately passes a rusted metal cover plate (Wp.14 122M) and heads downhill to the left of the trees where we meet water and are faced with stepping stones over **Butter Brook** (Wp.15 128M). This is a lovely picnic spot, not least because just up the far incline are several hut circles - what a great location for a settlement!

Past the remains, we meet a broad track leading to the reservoir where we turn left to rejoin our car tucked away in the car park (Wp.16 135M).

This short walk climbs the hillside behind **Ivybridge**, taking in the views down to the South Devon coast and the moors behind and then returns alongside the dramatic **River Erme** as it cascades off the moor through a beautifully wooded valley. Ideal for an afternoon stroll!

Note that sections of the walk may be very wet and difficult to negotiate after heavy rain.

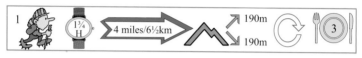

Access by car:
From the A38 turn off to **Ivybridge** on the B3213 towards the town centre, turn right at the roundabout by the **Methodist Church** and at the next roundabout turn left and park in the carpark.

We leave the carpark (Wp.1 0M) on the **Two Moors Way** to walk through the town with the **River Erme** on our left. Crossing directly over **Exeter Road** onto a riverside footpath, we take a bridge left (Wp.2 4M) over the river then immediately turn right onto **Station Road**. We follow the road gently uphill passing a school and a park on the left, bending left past a factory entrance then right uphill alongside the **Ivybridge Community Woodland**. Passing under an impressive viaduct, we climb more steeply and after 150 yards take a narrow muddy path on the left signed 'Henlake Down' (Wp.3 13M) into woodland, soon passing through a short tunnel.

The path between Wps. 5 & 6

We emerge from the woods (Wp.4 18M) through a gate onto moorland to continue on a grassy path through gorse and bracken, bearing right to gain height steadily towards the hill top. As we approach the brow we bear left to a gate (Wp.5 27M) leading onto a well-used footpath between high stone walls which takes us onto **Hanger Down** (Wp.6 32M).

We follow the hedge on our left until, reaching a small covered reservoir, we head north up across the well grazed pasture aiming for the crest of the hill and keeping **Hanger Down Clump** on our left, with good views of **Western Beacon** and **Butterdon Hill** on our right. Continuing north and gently down we gradually converge with the boundary hedge on our right which we follow as it bends right downhill (Wp.7 47M). Lovely views of **Harford Church** nestling below **Harford Common** open up in front of us as we look across the **Erme Valley**.

We follow a track downhill alongside a wall on our right, passing through one gate (Wp.8 49M) then turning right through the wall at another (Wp.9 52M) and immediately left following the 'Ivybridge via Erme Valley' sign.

The River Erme

The well-marked path becomes progressively wetter as we descend over a couple of stiles and then a set of stepping stones down into the heavily wooded valley and the **River Erme** (Wp.10 57M). (N.B. GPS reception is poor here.)

Heading off right (S) along the river bank, we pick our way with nifty footwork through boggy patches.

Just after a stile (Wp.11 67M) the path is diverted right, away from the river, round a particularly wet area where it's necessary to pick your way over stones, roots and other improvised 'dry islands' if you want to retain clean boots! We negotiate a ladder stile (Wp.12 72M) carrying straight on to rejoin the river as it now cuts its way dramatically down the valley through waterfalls and rapids. Picnic areas and well-sited gym apparatus (for those with excess energy to burn) provide opportunities to stop and enjoy the scene.

The viaduct looms ahead as the valley steepens and we divert left on a small track passing between two of the pillars (Wp.13 93M) then down a few steps across a small *leat* back to the river as it rushes through a steep gorge. We follow the track as it levels out exiting the woods onto **Station Road** by the factory entrance (Wp.14 100M) from where we retrace our steps downhill to the carpark (Wp15 108M) and perhaps to refreshment in **Ivybridge**.

For a neat little introduction to **Dartmoor** walking look no further! We have an easy climb onto open moorland with glorious views, a hint of history, the option of a good pub on the way round and finally, a delightful river walk to bring us back to our car. Perfect!

Note: the stepping stones on this route may not be passable after heavy rain.

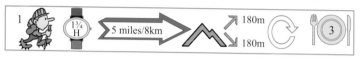

1 | 1¾ H | 5 miles/8km | 180m / 180m | ↻ | 3

Access by car:
From the B3212 **Princetown** to **Moretonhampstead** road, turn at **Two Bridges** on the B3357 towards **Dartmeet**. After 2 miles park on the left by **Dunnabridge Pound**.

Dunnabridge Pound

After investigating the beautifully formed **Dunnabridge Pound** (Wp.1 0M) we leave west, near the farm and through a gate (Wp.2 3M) into **Brownberry Newtake**. Our blue waymarked path is signed 'Laughter Hole Farm' and we bear right on the old stone track that quickly takes us up onto open moorland.

Carrying straight on at a gate (Wp.3 9M) we can appreciate the far-reaching views as we approach, then go through a couple of stone gateposts, passing disused mine shafts on our right.

Fifty yards further on we turn right (Wp.4 15M) down a broad track (SSE) with long grass and gorse either side, arriving in 8 minutes at **Outer Huccaby Ring** (Wp.5 23M). It's not one of the more imposing prehistoric enclosures on **Dartmoor**, but the gorse growing from the stones gives it its own charm as we follow the

eastern edge briefly before striking off south still on our track. We have an easy stroll on through a small wooden gate and then up to **Huccaby Tor** (Wp.6 29M) - petite with pretty views, before ambling down to the road at **Huccaby Tor Cottage** and turning left (Wp.7 36M).

Huccaby Tor

A careful four-minute walk on the B3357 (although there is the possibility of a somewhat overgrown path off to our right after 100 yards over rough land) brings us to **Hexworthy Cross** where we turn right down the lane to **Hexworthy** (Wp.8 40M); just past **Huccaby Farm** we come to a chapel with a chimney!

Dedicated to St. Raphael, it was built in 1869 by the Rector of Lydford as a mission chapel doubling as a schoolhouse on weekdays. It's worth a look inside to see the hearth and scholars' desks complete with inkwells, now used as pews.

St. Raphael's

Keeping straight on, we're joined by the lovely **West Dart River** to our right which we cross at **Hexworthy Bridge**, then negotiate a stone stile on the right into a field (Wp.9 52M). Yellow waymarks direct us diagonally up and across the field; below on our left is the rear of **Jolly Lane Cot**, reputedly the last house in England to be constructed in one day, thus allowing the builders to claim owners' rights. We tackle a couple more stiles across the meadow to carry straight on at the gate into the farmyard and leave it again onto a lane, faced by **Thimble Hall** cottage (Wp.10 60M).

Here we can make a brief diversion on the left to **The Forest Inn**, 'muddy paws and boots welcome' (Wp.11 64M), then retrace our steps to **Thimble Hall**, this time curving past it to the left.

The track splits as we follow the concrete to the left and, as it becomes private, we continue uphill on a narrow grassy path. The terrain opens out and we cross a tarmac track leading to a house before meeting a lane at a T-junction (Wp.12 74M). Turning right over a cattle grid, we can pick out the remains of the disused **Gobbett Tin Mine Tunnel** on our left as we drop down to cross the **River Swincombe** at the bridge (Wp.13 83M).

Just a few yards on the right is a blue waymarked gate leading to a public bridlepath and a set of stepping stones across the river, an idyllic spot to relax and daydream, lulled by the river babbling over stones while fish jump and

Stepping stones over Swincombe

dragonflies dance.

We set off on the well-trodden path alongside the river in this charming, secluded valley, nimbly negotiating the odd boggy patch before the **River Swincombe** joins the **West Dart River** in a stunning setting (Wp.14 91M).

Thirty-two massive granite blocks take us across to a beautiful spot, perfect for a picnic/swim/paddle/play/snooze - what

you will - which we sadly leave, going straight on with the **River Dart** alongside on our left. The grassy track finally leads us up through a wooden gate (Wp.15 103M) and on to the road (Wp.16 107M) where we turn left back to our car in the car park (Wp.17 108M).

West Dart stepping stones

This short walk tests balance and nerve, as we seek out and negotiate three sets of stepping stones around the famous **Dartmeet** area - great fun for young and old alike. After two exhilarating crossings of the tranquil **West Dart**, we head north past the ancient tenement farm at **Brimps** to negotiate the rushing **East Dart**. Our return, with a climb over **Yar Tor**, rewards us with aerial views of this picturesque countryside. A lovely stroll but a word of warning; this walk may not be possible after heavy rain!

2	2¼ H	5½ miles/9km	↗ 320m ↘ 320m	3

Access by car:
From the B3212 **Princetown** to **Moretonhampstead** road, turn at **Two Bridges** on the B3357 to **Dartmeet**. After 4 miles turn left into the **Dartmeet** car park.

Shortcut
To avoid the climb over **Yar Tor** follow the walk to Wp. 13. Cross the clapper bridge and turn right, following the stream down to the **East Dart**. Turn left, returning with the river to **Dartmeet** (1 hour 50 mins, 4½ miles 7km).

Extension
This walk can be extended by combining it at Wp.11 with Walk 10 (**Postbridge**).

From the car park (Wp.1 0M) we head to the road past the ancient **Dartmeet** clapper bridge with its missing central span, and turn right over the more modern bridge, climbing out of the **Dart** valley. After 50 yards, at an old petrol station (the antique pump still at the side of the house) we turn left (Wp.2 4M) following a sign for 'Holne Rd or Combestone Tor via Stepping Stones' and pass through a gate on the right hand side of the building.

Dartmeet stepping stones

A notice warns us that after heavy rain it may not be possible to cross the river via the stones. The path skirts the back of the building and we head left back down the hill to the **West Dart River** and our first set of stepping stones which we carefully cross; some of the gaps were made for people with a long stride!

Safely across, we carry straight on following the path through gorse bushes then up a small hill through a wooded area into well grazed fields - there's a good example of a *sheep creep* here (see photo on next page). We continue onwards following the wall on our left heading for a farm track ahead.

At the track (Wp.3 17M), which comes from **Combestone Farm** on our left, we carry straight on, climbing gently with lovely views of **Combestone Tor** and **Holne Moor** ahead. At the brow of the hill we pass a shed on the left and

cross a cattle grid, staying on the track; after 200 yards we arrive at another wall and cattle grid (Wp.4 22M) where we turn right following a sign to 'Week Ford'.

We make our way downhill into the **West Dart Valley** on the well-marked path. Through a gate, we follow the river bank to a delightful grassy haven in the sharp bend of the river at **Week Ford** (Wp.5 34M), where we find our second set of handsome stepping stones with the river surging between them.

Nimbly negotiating the crossing, we turn right for a few yards along the bank then leave the river following a marked narrow earthy path uphill between high hedges. Nearing the crest of the hill, we carry straight on along a broader track, then descend gently towards the buildings of **Huccaby Farm**.

Nimbly negotiating Week Ford

We follow the track which swings left past the farmyard and down to a road where we turn right (Wp.6 48M) to climb gently up to a T-junction with the main road that runs to **Dartmeet** (Wp.7 53M) at which we turn right, thankful that there's easy, safe walking along the right hand verge. After 100 yards we turn left off the road, into the driveway entrance to 'Brimpts' forestry commission plantation and **Brimpts Farm** (Wp.8 55M).

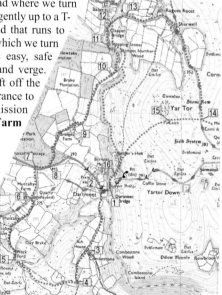

Our footpath takes us along the track to the farm (refreshments available during the summer season) where we are diverted left to skirt around the back of the main house and conference facilities.

Dolly's Cot (Wp.10)

Through a gate, we turn right, and after 50 yards are back again on track, now turning left (Wp.9 63M). The **East Dart Valley** is on our right, as we stride out downhill on a broad path across lush pasture, towards a gate and ruined cottage known locally as **Dolly's Cot** (Wp.10 71M). We're nearly down at river level, and keeping straight on to the river bank, we turn left upstream in a heavily wooded area. Following the river as it swings gently west, we soon see our third set of stepping stones defiantly taming the river and a sign indicating our way across the stones to **Babeny Road** (Wp.11 79M), following the course of a small tributary.

The path is well defined, as we head north between the stream on the right and wall on the left - a very pretty section. Soon we turn right over a small clapper bridge (Wp.12 85M) and head uphill, following the stream on our left as it cuts its way through a grassy meadow (a fine place for a picnic). Towards the edge of the field we cross another mini-clapper bridge and, joining an unfenced lane (Wp.13 89M), turn right uphill. We pass **Rogues Roost** on our left and continue through **Sherwell** on to **Corndon Down**, heading for the saddle between **Yar Tor** and **Corndon Tor** (Wp.14 112M). Impressive views start to open up as we climb, and a stone cross (Memorial to Lieutenant Cave-Penny killed in Palestine during WW1) appears on the skyline on our left. As we reach the saddle, we turn right on a broad path leading up to **Yar Tor**, our next destination (Wp.15 121M).

From the **Yar Tor** cairn we have a marvellous panorama. In the foreground we look down on **Dartmeet** and the **Dart Valley** and in the distance we have a 360 degree view of the moor and beyond. We leave the tor on a grassy path heading south-west down the steep slope in the direction of the **Dartmeet** car park below. On reaching the base of the hill we join a footpath and bear left along the side of **Badger's Holt** leading back to the car park (Wp.16 136M).

Refreshments can be found at **Badger's Holt**, or at a kiosk in the car park.

This pleasant walk is suitable for all types of weather. We start with a short stroll alongside the **River Dart**, then embark on a good climb on lightly trafficked country lanes and tracks onto the moor, followed by stunning views down into the picturesque **Dart Valley**. Our return path takes us along the famous **Dr Blackall's Drive** and onto bracken-lined paths, back down to the car park.

Access by car: From **Ashburton** follow the signs for the 'River Dart Country Park and Dartmeet'. Cross the **River Dart** at **Holne Bridge** and again at **New Bridge**. After 200 yards, fork right on the bend at **Barren Corner** down a narrow lane and after 100 yards, park on the left.

From the carpark (Wp.1 0M), we cross the lane and follow one of the many paths to the popular picnic and paddling place at a tight bend in the **River Dart** (Wp.2 3M). Here we turn left to walk along the riverside past a Pound hidden in the bracken on our left, rejoining the lane and turning right (Wp.3 9M). We climb a little, then level out and soon come to a fork (Wp.4 13M), where we bear left on a smaller lane, uphill to **Lower Town**.

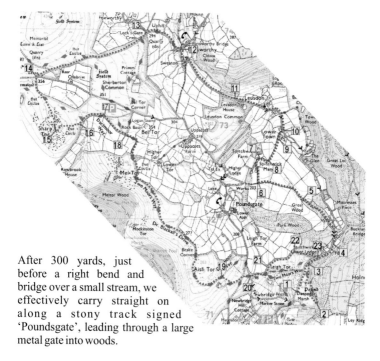

After 300 yards, just before a right bend and bridge over a small stream, we effectively carry straight on along a stony track signed 'Poundsgate', leading through a large metal gate into woods.

Still climbing, with a small brook running alongside us on the right, we enjoy tranquil woodland which we exit at a stile (Wp.5 23M) emerging into a well-grazed field.

Our path runs along the right by a hedge, then passes through the left-hand gate of a pair following yellow waymarks to join a small lane (Wp.6 30M), where we turn right towards the hamlet of **Spitchwick**. The lane skirts the grounds of the manor on our left, passing a shingle-clad cottage on the right. Just before **Spitchwick Farm**, at clump of bamboo, we turn right on a path helpfully signed 'pathway' (Wp.7 34M).

Through a small gate, we head directly ahead (E) and across a field to a second gate (Wp.8 36M) where we turn left to follow a hedge on the left across grazing pasture. At the corner of the field (Wp.9 41M) we take another gate onto a lane, past a secluded collection of picture-postcard cottages at **Lower Town**. We turn left uphill at a T-junction (Wp.10 43M), past **Leusdon Farm**, our road climbing steeply between high verdant hedges past **Leusdon Church** on the right. Ignoring a turning to the left, we carry straight on, turning right at a larger lane signed 'Ponsworthy' (Wp.11 53M).

We stride out downhill, the wooded **Webburn Valley** steeply down on our right. As we approach **Ponsworthy** at **Forder Bridge** (Wp.12 63M), we take a left turn, jumping over a small ford known as 'The Splash' (don't walk through the water unless good at skating!) and climb to a place appropriately named **Uphill**.

The Splash, at Forder Bridge

At **Locks Gate Cross** (Wp.13 70M) we carry straight on towards **Dartmeet** and start to reap the rewards for all that climbing, with great views of **Corndon Tor** on the right and later, **Sharp Tor** on our left.

The Dart Valley, from Wp.15

Passing **Sherrill Cross**, we continue to the junction with the main road (Wp.14 86M) and cross straight over, joining a grassy path through gorse. We follow a wall on our left, then head south-east directly up **Sharp Tor**, clambering over boulders as we get to the top (Wp.15 95M).

The views from here are stunning, the **Dart Valley** meandering below and a plethora of tors on the skyline. Heading east in the direction of the distant **Haytor Rocks**, we descend to a small lane (Wp.16 100M) and turn left, climbing out of a dip and hugging a boundary wall on the right.

Dr. Blackall's Drive

Dr. Blackall was the 19th century owner of **Spitchwick Manor** and is buried in **Leusdon** churchyard. He owned a great deal of the land in this area and had the driveway constructed after his wife became physically incapable of walking on the moor; their pony and trap could be seen regularly on fine days, making its way on the track.

We continue on a grassy path following the wall as it diverges right from the lane onto open moorland to our right (Wp.17 104M). After 300 yards a wall intersects from the left (Wp.18 108M) and we continue on a stony track with walls either side; after a further 150 yards we turn right now heading in the direction of **Mel Tor**. Joining the broad stony track known as **Dr. Blackall's Drive**, we contour along the top of the **Dart Valley** with **Bench Tor** rising up on the opposite side and the **Dart** rushing in the gorge below - a spectacular scene!

We follow the track as it half encircles **Aish Tor**, forking right at an obvious split (Wp.19 138M), on a closely cropped grassy track down through bracken. After 100 yards we turn left at a gravel track, cross a lane and come to a road (Wp.20 141M), heading straight across on a path past **Leigh Tor** pumping station and making our way downhill through tall bracken past **Leigh Tor** (Wp.21 144M).

Following closely to the hedge line, we come to private woodland and turn right just before the gate (Wp.22 151M), downhill to the road (Wp.23 157M) where we turn right back to the car park (Wp.24 163M).

Leats are fascinating waterways (there's a great book by Eric Hemery that's well worth reading if you're interested in exploring them) and this gentle figure of eight walk takes us along part of the well known **Holne Moor Leat;** also known as **Hamlyn's Leat.** With its source at the **O Brook**, it eventually joins with the **Holy Brook** to supply water to **Higher Buckfast Mill**. **Venford Reservoir**, one of Dartmoor's six water reserves, is petite but pretty and, last but not least, the **River Dart** has many and varied charms all of its own as it rolls from the moor down to the English Channel.

Not only do we experience these three on this walk (admittedly, the Dart from a distance) but we also happen upon a couple of splendid tors. **Combestone Tor** has the dubious claim to fame that it has the nearest carpark on Dartmoor (only 10 yards from car to tor), but it is none the less handsome for that, while **Bench Tor** offers superb views from its craggy outcrops.

Short Walk
The bigger loop – *leats*, ancient stones, a massive tor and views. We start at Wp.1 and follow though to Wp.13. This takes us to the road and across the dam and now we continue along the road to the car park on our left. (1¾ hours 4½ miles/7km)

Stroll
The smaller loop of the figure of eight – a quick climb, tors and views. From the car park we walk north along the road to Wp.13 turning right alongside the water treatment works. (45 minutes, distance 2 miles/3km)

Access by car: from **Ashburton** take the road signed 'River Dart Country Park' and 'Holne'. At **Butts Cross** (by **Holne**) take the 'Hexworthy and Venford Reservoir' signed road to arrive after 1.5miles at the car park on the right.

Leaving the car (Wp.1 0M), we cross the road to take the small path ahead, with the enclosed reservoir to our right and the moor to our left. After just 200 yards we gain access to the fenced area through a gate and turn left, enjoying the stroll along the water's edge to arrive shortly at a wooden footbridge (Wp.2 8M). A narrow track takes us up to the left through scrubby trees to quickly come to a metal boundary fence, which we clamber over helped by a stile (Wp.3 11M).

We set off (WNW) on a grassy track towards a tree struggling valiantly to survive, and soon pick up an ancient boundary wall on our left to guide us, the reservoir nestling below to our right. A small clapper bridge carries us over the dry **Wheal Emma** channel (Wp.4 17M) as we continue on the same bearing following a low *reave*, a larger wall spurring off to the left.

The lonely trees landmark

A couple of lonely trees on a hillock act as a useful landmark at this point – we aim just to the left of them. Keeping straight on, we come to a boundary line marked by a couple of stones and, as we cross, **Combestone Tor** appears to our right and a tall pillar of rock stands proud on the skyline ahead - **Horn's Cross**.

Our path is grassy amidst heathers, with increasingly splendid views as we make steady progress, onwards and upwards across the moor. A triple but indistinct stone row appears (Wp.5 29M) - not easy to spot the stones, even in winter - but the headstone juts up fairly clearly and it's worth a look.

Combestone Tor

Almost immediately, at two big rocks, we hit a large track and bear left making for the cross up on the hill. Arriving at the cross (Wp.6 34M), we savour the panoramic views. Now we head north towards **Combestone Tor** and over the boundary wall again, soon coming to the road - and there it is - a splendid lump of granite just itching to be climbed (Wp.7 46M).

Leaving the tor behind us we set off to the right (NW) along the road and a minute later turn right on a blue waymarked public footpath (Wp.8 52M), also the access to **Combestone Farm**. The gravel track swings right downhill leading us to a small bridge over **Holne Moor Leat** (Wp.9 58M) - this is the waterway that we will track back to the reservoir. **Dartmeet** is to the north but we bear right (E) following the flow of the leat, with **Yartor Down** rising on our left above the densely wooded **Dart Valley**.

Holne Moor Leat

We walk alongside the water in this tranquil setting, straying up to the road (Wp.10 79M) to avoid a boggy area and then rejoining the *leat* below on the left. A footpath to **Dartmeet** crosses our path but we continue past one hut circle on our right and then to a second (Wp.11 93M) - and here a lovely example of a *reave* runs away from the circle up the hill.

The *leat* now takes us gently on, passing **Luckey Tor** way below on our left - a good if somewhat scary looking climbing spot - as the **River Dart** wends its way (NE) through the trees; there are some interesting looking rapids down there with the occasional canoeist shooting by. We follow the *leat* until the reservoir comes into view and soon regain the road (Wp.12 106M) as the overflow water makes a dash for the brook below; an underground pipe takes the main flow under the dam roadway to emerge again just up the hill above our carpark! Our grassy path broadens as we turn left down to a carpark (not the one where we parked) to cross the dam on the road.

That completes the first part of our figure of eight as we prepare to strike out on our second loop. A sharp left turn directly after the dam (Wp.13 114M) takes us back along the side of the water treatment works and down almost to **Venford Brook** (Wp.14 118M). A broad stone-edged track contours round the hill and into oakwood where the trees hang with a wonderful variety of lichen, the ground strewn with comfy-looking mossy boulders.

By two big granite slabs (Wp.15 128M) a small track off to our right leads us up through the gnarled and twisted woodland - none of this contouring business now, just straight up - and we soon emerge to the first rocky outcrop of **Bench Tor** (Wp.16 135M). The panoramic view here is tremendous, from **Sharp Tor** opposite to the **Dart Valley** and round to **Holne Moor** - just superb!

The granite slabs at Wp.15

We have an 'upsy-downsy' section now as we head (S) towards the highest point on the tor (Wp.17 143M) and from this gorgeous but exposed spot relish the views once again. Following the well trodden path, we head (S) and then (SW) down the hill soon crossing the **West Stoke** spur of the **Holne Moor** *leat* (Wp.18 153M). We can pick out the left-hand corner of the conifers marking the reservoir and this guides us down to the road where we rejoin our car (Wp.19 156M).

Something of a challenge, this walk, especially if the weather's at all doubtful. A steady climb through pretty **Great Combe** brings us up to **Holne Ridge** - a wild, exposed area of typical moorland rewarding us with great views. We progress across rough terrain visiting the cairns on **Ryder's Hill**, **Snowdon** and **Pupers Hill** and a GPS is just brilliant for making life easy! A steady descent to a lovely picnic spot at **Chalk Ford** and a gentle stroll back to the car make for an exhilarating excursion.

5 · 3¼ H · 9 miles/14½km · 420m / 420m · 3

Access by car: From **Ashburton**, follow the signs to **Buckfast** and the 'River Dart Country Park and Holne'. ¾ mile after **Holne Bridge** turn left to **Holne** and 1¼ miles further on, turn left again at **Butts Cross**. Continue straight across at the next junction, signed 'free parking' and 'Scoriton' and follow the road round to the left past **Littlecombe**, arriving in **Scoriton**. Park on the road just past the pub.

Leaving the car (Wp.1 0M) we retrace our steps along the lane towards **Holne**, eyeing up the likely looking **Tradesman's Arms** on the right for a possible visit on our return. We drop down over **Holy Brook** to begin our ascent, turning left at **Littlecombe** (Wp.2 5M) signed 'the Dartmoor Way' along a country lane to **Michelcombe**. At this lovely secluded village we go left at the white signpost (Wp.3 13M) on a bridleway past **Inglett's Farm** on our right.

the ford at Wp.5

As the road surface breaks up to a stony track at a junction, we take to the right to 'Holne Moor via Great Combe' (Wp.4 16M). Through a metal gate, we're faced with a ford and footbridge just to the right (Wp.5 19M).

Crossing the water, we strike out left on a grassy track, the stream on our left, continuing up this pretty *combe* and straight on through a wooden gate, until the path (now stony) curves away right and approaches a small cottage on the right.

A blue waymarked post opposite (Wp.6 27M) directs us left, sharply uphill on a narrow, steepish, bracken-clothed path and through a couple of gates to a boundary wall with a little summer house on the left (Wp.7 31M). Leaving trees and shelter behind, we head straight on (N) onto the open moor and, meeting a *leat* (Wp.8 37M), cross it and follow it (N) for a few yards. We then cross another *leat* over two wooden planks, past a couple of inspection tanks and meet a large track head on (Wp.9 39M).

The bracken clothed path

Turning left on this broad pathway, well used by horse and hiker alike, we step out (WNW) towards **Holne Moor**, the *leat* parallel to us on our left, with good views to either side.

As we reach the top of a slight hill, always following the watercourse, a big track joins us from the right and together we cross a dried-up *leat*, with a sign 'farmer's water supply' on the left and come to a wooden footbridge where we swing left over the water (Wp.10 46M).

We follow the broad gravel track around to the right, keeping right after 3 minutes on a broad grassy track (Wp.11 49M), as the main path curves left and downhill.

The wall on our left guides us gently up through gorse and, contouring round **Holne Lee**, we have the hill on our right, the valley below on the left with a patchwork of fields beyond and the vast expanse of **Snowdon** looming directly in front (SW).

At the corner of the wall (Wp.12 53M), and with a mining *gert* coming down from the right, we enjoy level easy walking (SW) and continue straight on, any of a number of paths bringing us to **Sandy Way** directly in front of us (Wp.13 59M).

We turn right up the wide cropped grassway to the top where two low mounds either side of the track take us to a rectangular bound stone (Wp.14 68M), a broad path coming in from the right.

Following this track to the left, a second stone is quickly apparent; it's worth spending a couple of minutes here, enjoying fabulous all-round views, **Haytor Rocks** visible away in the distance (NE).

The lone tree

Mining *gerts* are obvious on the hillside ahead and we set off towards the one to the left, garnished with a lone tree (W), appreciating just how bald and bleak it is up here. From the gnarled, twisted hawthorn the track points us on (NW) to a couple more stones (Wp.15

On Ryder's Hill

77M); we continue steadily climbing **Holne Ridge** alongside disused tin workings, with **Venford Reservoir** visible to the right. Approaching the top, we come to a cross-tracks and turn left (Wp.16 84M SW).

Contouring on this broad grassy track we see mounds on the right and bear right just past them (Wp.17 88M W), going round the hill. The path narrows, taking us through small boggy patches and up and down *gerts* - not particularly easy walking - and we then curve left and gradually uphill.

Bound Stones

By the 12th century the boundaries of the **Forest of Dartmoor** with its neighbouring twenty-two parishes were probably clearly set. **Holne** was one such parish, and stones would have been put up to separate it not only from the forest, but also to mark the boundaries between the adjoining parishes of **Buckfastleigh** and **Widecombe**. We come across several bound stones during this walk - the leaning stone just north of Ryder's Hill is known as Little Anthony and is inscribed with 'H' for **Holne**. On the summit of **Ryder's Hill** we find two bound stones - the taller is marked 'B' for **Buckfastleigh** and is referred to as Petre's Bound Stone while the smaller is called Petre on the Mount and carries an 'H'. The old custom of 'Beating the Bounds', where parish boundaries were walked, ensured local knowledge of stones and routes was passed down the generations, a practice that still takes place in some areas today.

At a few boulders we meet a track and turn left (Wp.18 99M S), gently uphill on boggy land, passing a leaning bound stone from where we can pick out the trig point on **Ryder's Hill** (Wp.19 108M).

From the summit, we bear left (SE) on an indistinct path (possibly a vehicle may have been along here at some time) over tumpy grass and across wet peaty ground towards the two cairns on **Snowdon** (Wp.20 125M). There's not much shelter to be found here (but great views as usual) and we continue past another cairn (Wp.21 127M SSE) on a clearer, drier path through some *gerts* and into the saddle between **Snowdon** and **Pupers Hill**.

A short climb, and we're up by **Pupers Rock** (Wp.22 139M) and after a short stop, take the fairly obvious grassy path (SE) down again, soon coming to a cross-tracks (Wp.23 144M).

We follow to the left (NE), still descending, and where the track splits by a hawthorn set in boulders (Wp.24 148M) we stick to our bearing and fork right.

Losing height, we gain bracken, gorse and heather and at the corner of a wall, **Lud Gate** (Wp.25 154M), cross a stream to the left and then stroll round to the right keeping close to the wall on our right. Our path descends steadily through intrusive gorse, but eventually we ford a shallow stream and drop down on a broader stony track to **Chalk Ford** (Wp.26 167M).

Chalk Ford

Now, here's a pleasant spot for rest and recovery before negotiating the footbridge, turning right for **Scoriton** through a gate and following the track for a straightforward return to our car (Wp.27 192M).

Shipley Bridge is a great spot to start a walk - the **River Avon** tumbles over rocks through a rhododendron framed gorge and the paddling looks most inviting. But for this expedition we head off to the open moor via the **Avon Dam** and reservoir to look at the defunct **Red Lake** China Clay Works. We investigate an older landmark, **Petre's Cross**, then enjoy a steady return trip along the **Zeal Tramway** which takes us down from **Brent Moor**, with some lovely views for company.

4	3¾ H	9½ miles/15km	300m 300m	↻	0

Access by car:

From A38 take the B3372 to **South Brent** following the signs to the village centre, then take the road right signed 'Didworthy and Avon Dam'. Over the railway bridge turn immediately left signed 'Shipley Bridge' and at **Oakhill** fork left to **Didworthy**. At a crossroads carry straight on, then right at the next T-junction, still following signs to 'Didworthy'. Fork right at **Binamore Cross** then straight on at the next cross roads signed to 'Shipley Bridge', parking on the left just before the bridge.

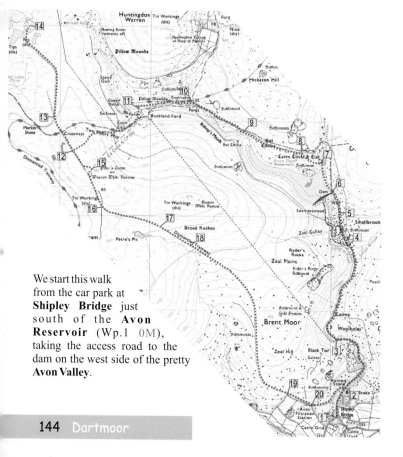

We start this walk from the car park at **Shipley Bridge** just south of the **Avon Reservoir** (Wp.1 0M), taking the access road to the dam on the west side of the pretty **Avon Valley**.

Hunter's Stone

The road climbs gently and meanders round the twists and turns of the river passing a road junction and large stone boulder known as **Hunters' Stone** on the left - a memorial to four fox hunting friends whose names appear on the sides (Wp.2 5M).

Avon Dam

Continuing, we cross the river at a stone bridge (Wp.3 15M) and stroll through open moorland catching our first glimpses of the **Avon Dam** as we pass water works at the riverside. As we approach the dam the road bears left to its base but we fork right (Wp.4 29M) on a broad grassy track towards the top.

Avon Reservoir

Climbing steadily, we cross remnants of an old railway (Wp.5 36M) and reach the concrete dam (Wp.6 39M) to see the reservoir beyond.

Following the track, we step out parallel with the water and can clearly see the conical tip of **Red Lake** spoil heap in line with the end of the lake. We cross **Brockhill Stream** (Wp.7 47M) and climb 300 yards up the slope to join the **Abbot's Way** a distinct path coming in from the right (Wp.8 53M). Continuing, we contour up the valley passing the reservoir end (Wp.9 63M), then drop down to a flat plain at river level on a gravel path. After crossing **Western Wella Brook** we come to one of the many **Abbot's Way** markers, **Huntingdon Cross**, beside a wall and gate (Wp.10 75M).

The clear path follows the river crossing it at a shallow ford (Wp.11 86M) just as the river bends right up the valley. (Note: If the water is high, use the clapper bridge crossing 300 yards up stream.) Over the river, we strike off on a grassy track (SW), following a mining *gert* uphill in line with the stone pillar of **Petre's Cross** on the hillside above. The *gert* gradually swings right as we climb levelling out as we reach the brow of the hill where we continue (WSW) reaching the course of the old **Zeal Tramway**, built in 1847 to take peat from **Red Lake** to **Shipley Bridge** (Wp.12 105M).

Turning right, (NW) we follow the course of the old railway downhill, seeing the occasional remains of granite sleepers, past old china clay settling pits on the left to intersect with the larger disused **Red Lake Tramway** (Wp.13 110M) where we turn right. Now we stride out along the broad track, through cuttings to the **Red Lake** china clay quarry, an idyllic spot on a good summer's day with a pretty lake and conical spoil heap - a great viewing point providing a magnificent 360 degree panorama (Wp.14 122M).

Retracing our steps along **Red Lake** and **Zeal Tramways** to Wp.12, we continue (SE) along the old track diverting left to **Petre's Cross** standing precariously on top of a stony cairn (Wp.15 153M).

Red Lake China Clay Quarry Pit

The spoil mound at Red Lake, the 'sky tip', is a useful landmark in fairly featureless countryside and was created over the years as china clay was extracted from the surrounding area. Of the three 'lakes' visible the largest is the quarry pit, the two smaller ones to the east being storage ponds. The works being supported by the **Red Lake Tramway** running for 8 miles down to near **Ivybridge**. The single line track carried up to a hundred workers at a time to the site from 1912 to 1932; the clay itself, however, was cleaned nearby and then piped off the moor for processing.

Petre's Cross

The views from the cairn are stunning, spanning the South Devon coast from **Torbay** to **Plymouth**.

The level track now takes us across the moor, with the **Red Lake Tramway** skirting round the hillside below. At a fork in the track (Wp.16 163M) we bear left and start to drop down the left hand side of a valley, mine workings on our right, still seeing the occasional granite sleeper to remind us that we're on the tramway.

The gentle decline makes for easy walking and we see the track curving round the side of **Brent Moor** ahead. Along the way a puzzling marker stone on the left of the track suggests that we are two miles from somewhere (Wp.17 173M), followed 500 yards further on by a stone inscribed with ' ¾ '(Wp.18 177M). Eventually we reach the corner of a boundary wall for the **Avon Filtration Plant** (Wp.19 205M) which we follow (SE) through tall gorse down to a metalled lane (Wp.20 210M). Going left, downhill, we join the road to **Avon Dam** at **Hunters' Stone** (Wp.2) and turn right to retrace our steps to the carpark (Wp.21 220M).

See the notes on Using GPS on Dartmoor on page 17.

1

YES TOR

Wp	Zo	East	North
1	SX	56093	91869
2	SX	56273	91626
3	SX	56593	92064
4	SX	56880	91888
5	SX	57871	91364
6	SX	58044	91242
7	SX	58248	91382
8	SX	58721	91573
9	SX	58991	91338
10	SX	59178	91168
11	SX	59022	91150
12	SX	59021	90696
13	SX	57920	90042
14	SX	57996	90222
15	SX	57932	89297
16	SX	58532	88211
17	SX	57901	87540
18	SX	56759	88741
19	SX	56223	89461
20	SX	55493	90719
21	SX	56060	91839
22	SX	56805	90754

2

SOURTON, & BRANSCOMBE'S LOAF

Wp	Zo	East	North
1	SX	54170	91209
2	SX	53506	90353
3	SX	53900	90162
4	SX	53587	89667
5	SX	54370	89589
6	SX	54475	89479
7	SX	55081	89195
8	SX	55205	89200
9	SX	55675	89873
10	SX	55482	90311
11	SX	55416	90360
12	SX	56050	91816
13	SX	56324	92160
14	SX	56408	92352
15	SX	56409	92413
16	SX	56416	92463
17	SX	56449	92478
18	SX	54457	91548
19	SX	54173	91194
20	SX	54766	89900
21	SX	54519	89677
22	SX	54596	90237

3

EAST OKEMENT RIVER & BELSTONE TOR

Wp	Zo	East	North
1	SX	59168	94535
2	SX	59399	94365
3	SX	59526	94355
4	SX	60260	94718
5	SX	60628	94199
6	SX	60715	93493
7	SX	60873	93845
8	SX	60923	93073
9	SX	61039	92937
10	SX	61137	92904
11	SX	60613	92225
12	SX	60505	92215
13	SX	60666	92138
14	SX	60883	92095
15	SX	60925	91698
16	SX	61148	91644
17	SX	61649	91515
18	SX	61937	93073
19	SX	61944	93689
20	SX	61793	93642
21	SX	61151	94312
22	SX	60613	94873
23	SX	60264	94970
24	SX	60200	94834
25	SX	59158	94535
26	SX	61525	93392

4

WIDGERY CROSS & GREAT LINKS TOR

Wp	Zo	East	North
1	SX	52456	85432
2	SX	53181	85267
3	SX	53312	85296
4	SX	53856	85663
5	SX	54017	85254
6	SX	54013	85178
7	SX	54127	84930
8	SX	54358	84920
9	SX	54986	84318
10	SX	55432	85356
11	SX	55618	86177
12	SX	55636	86443
13	SX	55007	86843
14	SX	55639	86587
15	SX	55873	86558
16	SX	55800	86743
17	SX	55547	87197
18	SX	54465	88786
19	SX	53528	87279
20	SX	52909	86398
21	SX	52864	86263
22	SX	52982	85783
23	SX	53067	85789
24	SX	52462	85445
25	SX	55055	86193

5

TAVY CLEAVE

Wp	Zo	East	North
1	SX	51731	83532
2	SX	52138	83342
3	SX	52477	83367
4	SX	52575	83077
5	SX	53567	83461
6	SX	54495	82377
7	SX	54857	83076
8	SX	55963	83848
9	SX	55799	83986
10	SX	55297	83516
11	SX	55042	83502
12	SX	54871	83491
13	SX	54596	83210
14	SX	54403	83533
15	SX	53887	84187
16	SX	53709	84112
17	SX	51730	83529

6

PETER TAVY & THE LANGSTONE

Wp	Zo	East	North
1	SX	52083	77957
2	SX	52167	77927
3	SX	53497	78214
4	SX	53843	78325
5	SX	54180	78736
6	SX	54931	78817
7	SX	55413	79082
8	SX	56108	79410
9	SX	56553	79503
10	SX	56199	79833
11	SX	55070	80470
12	SX	54540	80615
13	SX	53692	80516
14	SX	53342	80441
15	SX	53072	80474
16	SX	52884	80355
17	SX	52070	79751
18	SX	51841	80153
19	SX	51719	80126
20	SX	51129	79159

Wp	Zo	East	North
21	SX	50789	78819
22	SX	50809	78644
23	SX	50932	78534
24	SX	51145	77832
25	SX	51229	77816
26	SX	51313	77669
27	SX	51447	77714
28	SX	51775	77738
29	SX	51759	77915
30	SX	52089	77950

7
GREAT MIS & GREAT STAPLE TORS

Wp	Zo	East	North
1	SX	55980	74985
2	SX	56367	76373
3	SX	56279	76618
4	SX	56243	76864
5	SX	56168	76990
6	SX	56193	77191
7	SX	56228	77691
8	SX	55907	77844
9	SX	56384	78235
10	SX	56462	78269
11	SX	56479	78512
12	SX	55538	78279
13	SX	55495	78047
14	SX	54250	76673
15	SX	54121	76097
16	SX	53962	75725
17	SX	54445	75377
18	SX	54454	75136
19	SX	55066	75095
20	SX	55212	74837
21	SX	55974	74982

8
BEARDOWN MAN & WISTMAN'S WOOD

Wp	Zo	East	North
1	SX	60829	75128
2	SX	60627	75058
3	SX	60227	75369
4	SX	60345	75693
5	SX	60737	76058
6	SX	60766	76801
7	SX	60656	76956
8	SX	60428	77468
9	SX	60349	77761
0	SX	60056	78029
11	SX	59850	78255
12	SX	59816	78315
13	SX	59713	78943
14	SX	59519	79709
15	SX	60510	79910
16	SX	60586	78480
17	SX	60642	78386
18	SX	60756	78315
19	SX	61127	77833

Wp	Zo	East	North
20	SX	61194	76791
21	SX	60824	75154

9
EAST DART FROM FERNWORTHY

Wp	Zo	East	North
1	SX	65856	83986
2	SX	65378	84128
3	SX	64015	84410
4	SX	63781	84130
5	SX	63716	83320
6	SX	63763	83247
7	SX	63225	83120
8	SX	62061	82553
9	SX	61902	81860
10	SX	62655	81152
11	SX	62795	80995
12	SX	63492	81470
13	SX	63834	81524
14	SX	63925	81033
15	SX	64326	80981
16	SX	64567	81217
17	SX	64705	81385
18	SX	65558	81598
19	SX	65951	81636
20	SX	65970	81982
21	SX	66019	82714
22	SX	66124	83028
23	SX	65912	83763
24	SX	65848	83985

10
POSTBRIDGE EXPLORING THE DART

Wp	Zo	East	North
1	SX	64575	78941
2	SX	64701	78976
3	SX	65021	77980
4	SX	65453	77504
5	SX	65543	77414
6	SX	65758	77423
7	SX	65896	76487
8	SX	65993	76536
9	SX	66319	75908
10	SX	66181	75826
11	SX	66118	75636
12	SX	66488	75296
13	SX	66570	74907
14	SX	67114	74778
15	SX	67091	74996
16	SX	67250	75134
17	SX	67833	74980
18	SX	68007	76360
19	SX	67515	77301
20	SX	67352	78584
21	SX	66752	78548
22	SX	66565	78378
23	SX	65026	78858
24	SX	64579	78938

11
BENNETT'S CROSS-CHALLACOMBE-GOLDEN DAGGER MINE

Wp	Zo	East	North
1	SX	67874	81669
2	SX	68631	81926
3	SX	69078	81802
4	SX	69417	81604
5	SX	69198	81230
6	SX	69300	79742
7	SX	69248	79589
8	SX	69128	79374
9	SX	68479	79474
10	SX	68288	79135
11	SX	68119	79494
12	SX	68083	80061
13	SX	68231	80427
14	SX	68378	80114
15	SX	68136	81048
16	SX	67337	81014
17	SX	67874	81669

12
HAMELDOWN & GRIMSPOUND

Wp	Zo	East	North
1	SX	71837	76967
2	SX	71711	76905
3	SX	72373	79364
4	SX	72005	80279
5	SX	71190	80770
6	SX	71199	80835
7	SX	69992	80962
8	SX	70209	80670
9	SX	70483	79982
10	SX	70480	79614
11	SX	70553	79293
12	SX	70736	78988
13	SX	70693	77656
14	SX	70681	77317
15	SX	71054	76986

13
NORTH BOVEY, EASDON TOR & BOWERMAN'S NOSE

Wp	Zo	East	North
1	SX	73896	83925
2	SX	73704	83838
3	SX	73205	83809
4	SX	72847	83726
5	SX	72417	83027
6	SX	72856	82389
7	SX	72855	82310
8	SX	73099	81963
9	SX	73188	81803
10	SX	73641	81745
11	SX	73154	79988
12	SX	73779	80071
13	SX	73996	80534

14	SX	74101	80468
15	SX	74607	80523
16	SX	74854	80722
17	SX	74921	80923
18	SX	74904	81254
19	SX	74815	81341
20	SX	74718	81641
21	SX	74857	81802
22	SX	74588	82332
23	SX	74439	82912
24	SX	73906	83920
25	SX	73269	82397
26	SX	73583	82543
27	SX	74061	82944

14
TEN TORS - THE EASY WAY

Wp	Zo	East	North
1	SX	73872	79289
2	SX	74181	79061
3	SX	74529	78829
4	SX	75119	78846
5	SX	75292	78711
6	SX	75560	78361
7	SX	75218	77766
8	SX	74985	77861
9	SX	74892	77625
10	SX	75045	77583
11	SX	75367	77442
12	SX	75695	77144
13	SX	75016	76452
14	SX	74710	76245
15	SX	74114	76176
16	SX	73745	76236
17	SX	73405	76049
18	SX	73532	76325
19	SX	73173	77443
20	SX	72967	77662
21	SX	72999	77974
22	SX	72833	78316
23	SX	72755	78693
24	SX	73339	77831
25	SX	73798	78009
26	SX	73862	78150
27	SX	74377	78271
28	SX	74013	78839
29	SX	73873	79269

15
AROUND ILSINGTON

Wp	Zo	East	North
1	SX	78442	76283
2	SX	78487	76202
3	SX	78961	76064
4	SX	79127	76325
5	SX	79345	76501
6	SX	79897	75798
7	SX	79418	75934
8	SX	79318	75978
9	SX	78389	75434

10	SX	78436	75233
11	SX	78331	75145
12	SX	79221	74829
13	SX	79502	74883
14	SX	80188	75063
15	SX	80210	74855
16	SX	80007	74785
17	SX	79997	74522
18	SX	79538	74227
19	SX	79490	74146
20	SX	78896	74211
21	SX	78115	74990
22	SX	78368	75426
23	SX	78429	76296

16
HAYTOR QUARRIES & THE TRAMWAY

Wp	Zo	East	North
1	SX	76442	77179
2	SX	75770	77171
3	SX	75936	77532
4	SX	75835	77554
5	SX	75997	77650
6	SX	76102	77826
7	SX	75959	78732
8	SX	76181	79043
9	SX	76511	78349
10	SX	76800	78151
11	SX	76956	77945
12	SX	77856	77434
13	SX	77799	77432
14	SX	77278	77247
15	SX	77079	77317
16	SX	77059	77310
17	SX	77021	77269
18	SX	76710	77361
19	SX	76447	77200

17
LUSTLEIGH CLEAVE - HUNTER'S TOR

Wp	Zo	East	North
1	SX	78852	80185
2	SX	78685	80288
3	SX	77918	80080
4	SX	77551	80611
5	SX	77401	80890
6	SX	77005	81191
7	SX	76999	81280
8	SX	77320	81667
9	SX	77008	81640
10	SX	75972	82562
11	SX	75830	82881
12	SX	75745	82930
13	SX	75684	82147
14	SX	75886	81904
15	SX	75799	81695
16	SX	75550	81469
17	SX	75818	80912

18	SX	76629	81144
19	SX	77555	80270
20	SX	77861	80054
21	SX	78216	79590
22	SX	78799	80176

18
LUSTLEIGH & BECKY FALLS

Wp	Zo	East	North
1	SX	78427	81340
2	SX	78079	81351
3	SX	78099	81199
4	SX	77891	81005
5	SX	77836	80988
6	SX	77641	80936
7	SX	77437	80942
8	SX	76948	81222
9	SX	76618	81181
10	SX	75842	80934
11	SX	75585	80795
12	SX	75617	80734
13	SX	75692	80259
14	SX	76266	80208
15	SX	76457	80372
16	SX	77159	80363
17	SX	77550	80273
18	SX	77846	80072
19	SX	77908	80137
20	SX	78254	80753
21	SX	78408	81340

19
TRENCHFORD RESERVOIR

Wp	Zo	East	North
1	SX	80355	82457
2	SX	80155	82959
3	SX	80077	83100
4	SX	80140	83446
5	SX	80229	83498
6	SX	80603	83671
7	SX	80627	83920
8	SX	80736	83954
9	SX	81188	84133
10	SX	81064	84446
11	SX	81681	84817
12	SX	81880	84859
13	SX	83007	85498
14	SX	83156	85125
15	SX	83164	85091
16	SX	82841	84769
17	SX	82413	84630
18	SX	82110	84677
19	SX	82193	84424
20	SX	82323	84068
21	SX	82228	83592
22	SX	81552	83538
23	SX	81280	83581
24	SX	80939	83371
25	SX	80916	82825

| | | 26 | SX | 80351 | 82466 |

20

STEPS TO CHAGFORD ALONG THE TEIGN

Wp	Zo	East	North
1	SX	80176	88408
2	SX	80416	88424
3	SX	78354	89345
4	SX	78140	89910
5	SX	77923	89790
6	SX	76844	90026
7	SX	76102	89832
8	SX	74211	90031
9	SX	72067	89640
10	SX	71207	89429
11	SX	70909	89107
12	SX	70519	88568
13	SX	70409	88317
14	SX	69882	88315
15	SX	69257	88084
16	SX	69319	87911
17	SX	69960	87616

21

THE TEIGN GORGE FROM FINGLE BRIDGE

Wp	Zo	East	North
1	SX	74210	90022
2	SX	74210	90188
3	SX	72730	90008
4	SX	71933	90224
5	SX	72087	89645
6	SX	72279	89046
7	SX	72581	88873
8	SX	72501	89240
9	SX	72421	89646
10	SX	72355	89569
11	SX	72799	89853
12	SX	74211	90025

22

MARDON DOWN & BLACKINGSTONE ROCK

Wp	Zo	East	North
1	SX	75268	86016
2	SX	75466	86113
3	SX	75639	86231
4	SX	75706	86323
5	SX	75899	86406
6	SX	76432	86545
7	SX	76556	86515
8	SX	76656	86800
9	SX	76709	86836
10	SX	76695	86990
11	SX	76976	87888
12	SX	77561	87939
13	SX	77927	88105
14	SX	78291	88107
15	SX	78291	87951

16	SX	78701	87629
17	SX	78403	87353
18	SX	78874	87134
19	SX	79684	86930
20	SX	78378	85683
21	SX	78550	85668
22	SX	78065	85594
23	SX	77675	85437
24	SX	77511	85610
25	SX	77525	85520
26	SX	76924	85408
27	SX	76158	85551
28	SX	75869	85804
29	SX	75261	86022

23

CHAGFORD & THE TWO HILLS

Wp	Zo	East	North
1	SX	70092	87519
2	SX	70872	87607
3	SX	70972	87451
4	SX	71069	87276
5	SX	71335	87095
6	SX	71426	86900
7	SX	71350	86752
8	SX	71252	86660
9	SX	71168	86567
10	SX	71271	86515
11	SX	71071	86606
12	SX	70653	86812
13	SX	70424	86727
14	SX	70238	86703
15	SX	70030	86757
16	SX	69957	86667
17	SX	69751	85725
18	SX	69472	86193
19	SX	69494	86332
20	SX	69649	86954
21	SX	69614	87176
22	SX	69593	87543
23	SX	70102	87514

24

KESTOR ROCK & SCORHILL CIRCLE

Wp	Zo	East	North
1	SX	66110	86626
2	SX	66070	86478
3	SX	66448	86353
4	SX	65937	85758
5	SX	65851	86090
6	SX	65269	87146
7	SX	65404	87169
8	SX	65360	87462
9	SX	65194	88743
10	SX	65204	88848
11	SX	66094	89298
12	SX	66222	89260
13	SX	66308	89677

14	SX	67214	89682
15	SX	67444	89361
16	SX	67370	88858
17	SX	67144	88415
18	SX	67263	88061
19	SX	66955	87590
20	SX	66841	87345
21	SX	66313	86920
22	SX	66115	86636

25

SOUTH ZEAL & COSDON HILL

Wp	Zo	East	North
1	SX	65096	93506
2	SX	65208	93301
3	SX	65157	93193
4	SX	65131	93087
5	SX	65118	92696
6	SX	65151	92358
7	SX	64977	92070
8	SX	64595	91876
9	SX	64305	91661
10	SX	64090	91180
11	SX	63759	90595
12	SX	63706	90471
13	SX	63359	90836
14	SX	63191	89689
15	SX	63183	90021
16	SX	63519	91573
17	SX	63616	91795
18	SX	63678	92512
19	SX	63667	93115
20	SX	64209	93135
21	SX	64468	93205
22	SX	64578	93283
23	SX	64735	93292
24	SX	65089	93506

26

ROUND FOXTOR MIRES

Wp	Zo	East	North
1	SX	60286	70884
2	SX	60813	70897
3	SX	60742	69851
4	SX	60653	69804
5	SX	60800	69802
6	SX	60961	69964
7	SX	61551	69993
8	SX	61563	70233
9	SX	61809	70078
10	SX	62476	70372
11	SX	62843	70348
12	SX	62860	70615
13	SX	62842	71033
14	SX	62911	71190
15	SX	62757	71429
16	SX	63382	71899
17	SX	63322	71987
18	SX	63257	72111

Wp	Zo	East	North
19	SX	64096	72556
20	SX	63402	72642
21	SX	61683	73055
22	SX	61145	73194
23	SX	61189	73151
24	SX	60326	73271
25	SX	60767	71948
26	SX	60817	71736
27	SX	60230	71059
28	SX	60317	70884

27
RAILWAYS & QUARRIES

Wp	Zo	East	North
1	SX	55961	74965
2	SX	55831	74738
3	SX	55478	74866
4	SX	55261	74673
5	SX	55067	75089
6	SX	54948	75108
7	SX	54850	73377
8	SX	54530	72343
9	SX	54889	72404
10	SX	55258	72246
11	SX	55602	73327
12	SX	55515	73463
13	SX	55634	74133
14	SX	56430	73290
15	SX	56636	75066
16	SX	55962	74969

28
DOUBLE WATERS & GRENOFEN BRIDGE

Wp	Zo	East	North
1	SX	48873	71009
2	SX	48932	71115
3	SX	48749	71079
4	SX	47952	70221
5	SX	47679	70136
6	SX	47513	69977
7	SX	47200	69900
8	SX	47473	69744
9	SX	47577	69111
10	SX	47858	69459
11	SX	48466	69950
12	SX	48656	69968
13	SX	48969	70447
14	SX	49344	70284
15	SX	49629	70355
16	SX	49930	70419
17	SX	48883	71022

29
FROM BURRATOR TO DRIZZLECOMBE

Wp	Zo	East	North
1	SX	56705	69470
2	SX	56746	69547
3	SX	56809	70039
4	SX	57276	70114
5	SX	57753	70152
6	SX	58163	70512
7	SX	58498	70440
8	SX	59725	70633
9	SX	60069	69956
10	SX	60379	70019
11	SX	60084	68553
12	SX	59772	68246
13	SX	59163	67878
14	SX	59083	67774
15	SX	59146	67443
16	SX	59290	67308
17	SX	59114	67073
18	SX	58955	66937
19	SX	58827	66673
20	SX	58296	66368
21	SX	57961	67433
22	SX	58026	67505
23	SX	57786	67806
24	SX	57400	67920
25	SX	57186	68276
26	SX	57028	68694
27	SX	56526	68976
28	SX	56706	69473

30
FOLLOWING THE DEVONPORT LEAT AT BURRATOR

Wp	Zo	East	North
1	SX	56775	69380
2	SX	56669	69462
3	SX	56431	69761
4	SX	56837	70965
5	SX	57166	71425
6	SX	57227	71464
7	SX	57380	71727
8	SX	57231	71889
9	SX	57426	71741
10	SX	57502	71764
11	SX	57634	71614
12	SX	57316	71414
13	SX	59726	70630
14	SX	59756	70064
15	SX	60069	69956
16	SX	59096	69535
17	SX	58926	69462
18	SX	58587	69338
19	SX	57882	69475
20	SX	57239	69394
21	SX	56775	69371

31
DEWERSTONE ROCK

Wp	Zo	East	North
1	SX	53230	63691
2	SX	53326	63616
3	SX	53756	63545
4	SX	54273	63945
5	SX	55011	64331
6	SX	55447	64705
7	SX	55241	64790
8	SX	54084	64242
9	SX	53690	63979
10	SX	53635	64376
11	SX	53484	64091
12	SX	53485	63843
13	SX	53246	63750
14	SX	53258	63690

32
AROUND BURRATOR RESERVOIR

Wp	Zo	East	North
1	SX	56773	69378
2	SX	56507	68974
3	SX	56828	68708
4	SX	56888	68303
5	SX	56555	68299
6	SX	56446	68324
7	SX	56298	68279
8	SX	55940	68165
9	SX	55813	68047
10	SX	55732	67837
11	SX	55805	67635
12	SX	55361	67488
13	SX	55215	67214
14	SX	55016	67007
15	SX	54525	66889
16	SX	54450	67059
17	SX	54344	67236
18	SX	53979	67266
19	SX	54054	67723
20	SX	54140	67846
21	SX	54168	68084
22	SX	54678	69326
23	SX	55171	69279
24	SX	55466	69457
25	SX	56053	69565
26	SX	56431	69762
27	SX	56649	69470
28	SX	56772	69385

33
WESTERN BEACON

Wp	Zo	East	North
1	SX	64247	59616
2	SX	65430	60447
3	SX	65631	60528
4	SX	65693	60182
5	SX	65999	59550
6	SX	66649	59178
7	SX	66095	59095
8	SX	65445	58720
9	SX	65421	58209
10	SX	65332	57719
11	SX	65201	57526
12	SX	64809	57648
13	SX	65031	58328

Wp	Zo	East	North
14	SX	64728	58987
15	SX	64376	59278
16	SX	64245	59612

34
EXPLORING THE ERME VALLEY FROM IVYBRIDGE

Wp	Zo	East	North
1	SX	63520	56169
2	SX	63519	56433
3	SX	63481	57089
4	SX	63232	56971
5	SX	62797	57357
6	SX	62767	57605
7	SX	62619	58773
8	SX	62704	58848
9	SX	62867	58959
10	SX	63066	58992
11	SX	63212	58598
12	SX	63329	58376
13	SX	63507	57052
14	SX	63471	56723
15	SX	63512	56161

35
HUCCABY & HEXWORTHY

Wp	Zo	East	North
1	SX	64469	74686
2	SX	64456	74728
3	SX	64821	74964
4	SX	65206	75249
5	SX	65487	74567
6	SX	65590	74094
7	SX	65932	73660
8	SX	66299	73484
9	SX	65777	72960
10	SX	65343	72918
11	SX	65422	72721
12	SX	65016	72814
13	SX	64588	73215
14	SX	64714	73784
15	SX	64732	74457
16	SX	64601	74603
17	SX	64487	74660

36
DARTMEET STEPPING STONES

Wp	Zo	East	North
1	SX	67137	73332
2	SX	67045	73242
3	SX	66860	72631
4	SX	66764	72294
5	SX	66093	72493
6	SX	66262	73160
7	SX	66307	73477
8	SX	66426	73511
9	SX	66796	73962

Wp	Zo	East	North
10	SX	67130	74469
11	SX	67097	74807
12	SX	67095	74990
13	SX	67257	75127
14	SX	68130	73997
15	SX	67765	74016
16	SX	67158	73349

37
DR. BLACKALL'S DRIVE

Wp	Zo	East	North
1	SX	71195	71320
2	SX	71430	71197
3	SX	71328	71624
4	SX	71594	71802
5	SX	71269	72311
6	SX	70788	72469
7	SX	70796	72742
8	SX	70889	72715
9	SX	71000	72930
10	SX	71056	73031
11	SX	70530	73350
12	SX	69931	73859
13	SX	69552	74039
14	SX	68384	73585
15	SX	68565	73026
16	SX	68840	73086
17	SX	69085	73168
18	SX	69330	72963
19	SX	70383	71468
20	SX	70703	71482
21	SX	70894	71552
22	SX	71197	71756
23	SX	71452	71687
24	SX	71216	71335

38
AROUND HOLNE MOOR

Wp	Zo	East	North
1	SX	68743	70963
2	SX	68256	70748
3	SX	68208	70750
4	SX	67952	70846
5	SX	67342	71119
6	SX	66888	71114
7	SX	66918	71852
8	SX	66792	71913
9	SX	66747	72160
10	SX	67430	71484
11	SX	67937	71884
12	SX	68247	71368
13	SX	68685	71209
14	SX	68640	71497
15	SX	68771	72176
16	SX	68983	72000
17	SX	69074	71707
18	SX	68869	71160
19	SX	68748	70960

39
RYDER'S & PUPERS HILLS

Wp	Zo	East	North
1	SX	70299	68574
2	SX	70153	68918
3	SX	69566	69040
4	SX	69426	69002
5	SX	69344	69203
6	SX	69312	69451
7	SX	69285	69641
8	SX	69380	69855
9	SX	69386	69911
10	SX	69016	69987
11	SX	68847	69896
12	SX	68596	69774
13	SX	68332	69334
14	SX	67828	69699
15	SX	67155	69834
16	SX	66721	69944
17	SX	66521	69730
18	SX	65839	69741
19	SX	65883	69139
20	SX	66779	68363
21	SX	66812	68252
22	SX	67177	67451
23	SX	67514	67156
24	SX	67756	67282
25	SX	68204	67479
26	SX	68390	68159
27	SX	70301	68584

40
THE AVON DAM & RED LAKE QUARRY

Wp	Zo	East	North
1	SX	67946	62990
2	SX	68050	63254
3	SX	67975	63761
4	SX	68092	64763
5	SX	67994	65138
6	SX	67921	65325
7	SX	67792	65635
8	SX	67586	65764
9	SX	66950	65968
10	SX	66369	66264
11	SX	65761	66226
12	SX	65030	65788
13	SX	64842	66117
14	SX	64553	67064
15	SX	65256	65566
16	SX	65381	65158
17	SX	65997	64952
18	SX	66349	64750
19	SX	67430	63197
20	SX	67667	63076
21	SX	67966	63002

GLOSSARY

adit horizontal opening into a mine, used for drainage

beehive hut workmen's shelter or store house

blowing house medieval workshop for processing tin ore

bound stone (bond-stone) a boundary stone sometimes inscribed with the initials of a parish or landowner

Bronze Age stage between the Stone and Iron Ages (approx. 2500 BC to 500 BC when tools and weapons were made of bronze

burgage plot long strip of land in a medieval town or village running at right angles to the main street behind the properties

bund earth embankment

cairn rough pile of stones built as a landmark, memorial or tomb

cist box-shaped burial chamber made from stone slabs

cleave valley with steep sides

clitter scattered rockfield falling away from a *tor*

combe short valley or deep hollow

corbel stone supporting bracket

dolmen Neolithic tomb consisting of a horizontal stone supported by several vertical stones

drove road ancient road giving access to the high moor from the lowlands

gert surface cutting made by miners

hut circle circular remains of a simple thatch roofed stone dwelling

Iron Age period following the Bronze Age, about 500 BC to 50 AD

kistvaen (see *cist*)

leat man-made water channel

logan stone rocking stone

long-house traditional medieval dwelling with quarters for humans and animals

menhir single standing stone dating from the late Neolithic Bronze Age

mire area of soft, wet spongy ground formed by trapped rotting vegetation

Neolithic relating to the period from about 4000 BC to 2400 BC

newtake land taken into ownership from open moorland

pillow mound loose pile of earth created for rabbits to inhabit

pound enclosure, usually circular; a simple pound could hold only animals, a larger pound could contain a whole prehistoric settlement of up to 60 huts

reave low bank acting as a boundary in a field system dating from around 1500 BC, made from piled up earth or stones. *Reaves* may be many kilometres long and are generally laid out in dead straight lines.

rock basin natural hollow produced by weathering on a *tor* or by erosion in a river

sheep creep way through a stone wall for sheep

sheep leap crossing point for sheep over a *leat*

stannary relating to the medieval tin industry

stone circle Late Neolithic/Bronze Age circle of stones, possibly with ceremonial significance

stone row Late Neolithic/Bronze Age row of set stones often leading from a burial cairn or *cist* to a terminal stone (*menhir*). The longest known row in the world (4km) lies in the **Erme Valley** on southern Dartmoor.

tor prominent rock or heap of rocks

warren piece of land where rabbits were farmed commercially

APPENDICES

BIBLIOGRAPHY

Ancient Dartmoor - An Introduction Paul White
(Bossiney Books £2.99 ISBN 1-899383-22-0)

Medieval Dartmoor Paul White
(Bossiney Books £2.99 ISBN 1-899383-3-3)

The Making of Modern Dartmoor
(Bossiney Books £2.99 ISBN 1-899383-54-9)

Dartmoor 365 John Hayward
(Curlew Publications £9.99 ISBN 0-9514037-2-9)
A Field Guide to the Boundary Markers on and around Dartmoor Dave Brewer
(Devon Books £3.95 ISBN 0-86114-786-3)
The A to Z of Dartmoor Tors Terry Bound
(Obelisk Publications £4.95 ISBN 1-899073-27-2)
The Warren House Inn, Dartmoor Tom Greeves & Elisabeth Stanbrook
(Quay Publications £4.95 ISBN 1-870083-40-7)
Dark and Dastardly Dartmoor Sally and Chips Barber
(Obelisk Publications £1.95 ISBN 0-946651-98-1)
Walking the Dartmoor Waterways Eric Hemery
(Peninsula Press £7.99 ISBN 1-872640-13-3)
Water from the Moor David J. Hawkins
(Devon Books £4.95 ISBN 0-86114-788-X)
Dartmoor Stone Stephen H. Woods
(Devon Books ISBN 0-86114-843-6)

LOCAL PUBLICATIONS
Dartmoor Visitor free from Dartmoor National Park Authority
Dartmoor - The Country Magazine (Halsgrove Magazines, quarterly £2.50)
Dartmoor Magazine (Quay Publications, quarterly £2.50)
Dartmoor News (The Dartmoor Company, bi-monthly £2.50)

ORGANISATIONS & WEBSITES
Dartmoor National Park Authority
Parke, Haytor Road, Bovey Tracey, Newton Abbot, Devon TQ13 9JQ
01626 832093   www.dartmoor-npa.gov.uk
DNPA Information Centres:
Haytor   01364 661520   haytor@dartmoor-npa.gov.uk
Newbridge   01364 631303   newbridge@dartmoor-npa.gov.uk
Postbridge   01822 880272   postbridge@dartmoor-npa.gov.uk
Princetown   01822 890414   hmvc@dartmoor-npa.gov.uk
(The High Moorland Visitor Centre)
Tourist Information Centres:
Okehampton   01837 53020   www.okehampton-devon.co.uk
Tavistock   01822 612938   www.tavistock-devon.co.uk
Community Information Centres:
Ashburton   01364 653426   www.ashburton.org
Bovey Tracey   01626 832047   www.boveytracey.gov.uk
Buckfastleigh   01364 644522   www.buckfastleigh.org
Ivybridge   01752 897035
Moretonhampstead 01647 440043

**Dartmoor Preservation
Association**   01822 890646   www.dartmoorpreservation.com
Dartmoor Society   www.dartmoorsociety.com

Dartmoor Training 0800 458 4868   www.dartmoor-ranges.co.uk
Area (MOD)

National Trust   01392 881691   www.nationaltrust.org.uk
Devon Regional Office

Letterbox 100 Club 01392 832768   www.walk.to/letterboxing

**West Country
Tourist Board**   01392 425426   www.westcountrynow.com

PLACES OF INTEREST
Becky Falls   01647 221259   www.beckyfalls.com
Open daily April to October from 10 am

Buckfast Abbey,
Buckfastleigh   01364 645500   www.buckfast.org.uk

Canonteign Falls   01647 252434   www.canonteignfalls.com

Dartmoor Prison Heritage Centre HMP Dartmoor, Princetown
09.30-12.30 and 13.30-16.30 (16.00 Sundays and Fridays)
                         01822 892130   www.dartmoor-npa.gov.uk

Dartmoor Railway and Visitor Centre, Okehampton
                 01837 55637   www.dartmoorrailway.co.uk

Devon Guild of Craftsmen Riverside Mill, Bovey Tracey
Open 7 days 10.00-5.30 01626 832223   www.crafts.org.uk

Museum of Dartmoor Life, Museum Courtyard, 3 West St, Okehampton
Open Easter-October daily
                 01837 52295   www.museumofdartmoorlife.eclipse.co.uk

NATIONAL TRUST   www.nationaltrust.org.uk
Castle Drogo NT   01647 433306
Open: Castle March to October daily except Tues, 11.00-5.00
Garden daily throughout year 10.30-5.30 or dusk

Buckland Abbey NT   01822 853607
Open: March to October daily except Thurs, 10.30-5.30

Finch Foundry NT   01837 840046
Open: April to October daily except Tues, 11.00-5.30

Lydford Gorge NT   01822 820320/820441
Open all year - phone for opening times

TRANSPORT
Bus   www.transportdirect.info
Traveline   0870 6082608   www.traveline.org.uk
The 'Dartmoor Sunday Rover' allows unlimited travel on a selection of bus and train
routes across Dartmoor (£5 adult, £4 child, £4.50 senior citizen)
                 01392 382800 or 01837 54545
Train   www.dartmoorrailway.co.uk
Dartmoor Line Exeter to Okehampton (summer and Sundays only)
             01837 55637 or 01392 382800 - links with walk 3
The Dartmoor Railway: The Dartmoor Pony Okehampton Station to **Meldon**
Viaduct (weekends and holidays)
             01837 55637 - links with walks 2, 3

Walk! Wire-O Spiral Bound Guidebooks are designed to be used with:
- DWG's plastic slipcover (PSC), which prevents the binding from catching on
  pockets and increases durability -
- - and our clear plastic All Weather Book Bag (AWBB) with grip-top seal
  which allows the book to be folded back displaying 2 pages, then sealed,
  impervious to weather conditions.
To obtain your PSC and AWBB for this book, send a C5 (9 x 7 inch) SAE with 47p
stamp, to:
                    (Code 9781904946127)
                    Discovery Walking Guides
                    10 Tennyson Close
                    Northampton NN5 7HJ

Devon Bus N°	Route	Links with Walk N°s
48	**Wembury** to **Burrator**	29, 30, 32
56	Yelverton to Dousland	32
58, 59	**Plymouth** to **Lee Moor**	31
82	'Transmoor Link' runs across the moor from **Plymouth** to **Exeter** via **Princetown**, **Postbridge** and **Moretonhampstead**	8, 10, 11, 20, 22
86	**Plymouth** to **Barnstaple** via **Tavistock** & **Okehampton**	2, 4, 6
95	Horndon to Tavistock via Mary Tavy	6
98	**Tavistock** to **Yelverton** via **Princetown** & **Postbridge**	7, 8, 10, 27
118	Okehampton to Plymouth via Tavistock	2, 3, 4, 6
170	**Exeter** to **Totnes** via **Widecombe**	12, 14, 16
172	Tavistock to Totnes via Princetown, Dartmeet & Ashburton	7, 8, 10, 12, 14, 16, 27, 36
173	**Exeter** to **Moretonhampstead** via **Chagford**	21, 22, 23
174	Okehampton to Widecombe via Moretonhampstead	3, 12, 14, 16, 22
178	**Newton Abbot** to **Moretonhampstead**	18, 22
179	Okehampton to Totnes via Moretonhampstead and Newton Abbot	3, 21, 22, 25
187	**Okehampton** to **Gunnislake** via **Lydford** and **Tavistock**	2, 3, 4, 6
193	Haytor to Newton Abbot via Ilsington	14, 15, 16
359	**Exeter** to **Moretonhampstead** via **Dunsford**	20, 22
360	Bridford to Exeter via Christow	19
361	**Bridford** to **Newton Abbot** via **Christow**	19
670	Cheriton Bishop to Okehampton via Belstone	3, 24
671	**Okehampton** to **Newton Abbot** via **Manaton** & **Trago Mills**	3, 13, 22, 23
672	Buckland to Newton Abbot via Widecombe	12, 37, 39
893	Holne to Ashburton via Buckfastleigh	37, 39

INDEX OF PLACE NAMES